T5-DHR-785

Meeting Standards

Instructional Strategies for Struggling Students

Anne M. Beninghof, M.S.

Education Library
Sprague Technology Center

Copyright 2003 Sopris West
All rights reserved.

Permission is granted to the purchasing teacher to reproduce the forms contained within this book for use with his or her students only. No other part of this book may be reproduced without written permission from the publisher.

ISBN 1-57035-515-0

Illustration by Joyce Turley

Highlighter Tape® is a registered trademark of Dennison Manufacturing Company.
Hula Hoop® is a registered trademark of Wham-O, Inc.
Lego® is a registered trademark of Interlego A.G. Switzerland Corporation.
Nite Companion® is a registered trademark of KTS, Inc.
Rolodex® is a registered trademark of Berol Corporation.
Scrabble® is a registered trademark of Milton Bradley.
Unifix® is a registered trademark of Philograph Publications Limited.
Velcro® is a registered trademark of Velcro Industries B.U. Netherlands/Holland Corporation.
Wikki Stix® one-of-a-kind creatables is a registered trademark of Omnicor, Inc.

09 08 07 06 05   8 7 6 5 4

Printed in the United States of America
Published and Distributed by

SOPRIS
WEST™

EDUCATIONAL SERVICES

A Cambium Learning™ Company

4093 Specialty Place • Longmont, Colorado 80504 • (303) 651-2829
www.sopriswest.com

154MEET/10-05

Acknowledgments

I have the good fortune of knowing many excellent teachers. They include hundreds of students, parents, colleagues, and friends. I would especially like to thank all who have so willingly shared their ideas about teaching struggling students. It is through their generosity that this book is possible. Above all, my thanks to Joe, who has inspired me by continually holding, and striving to reach, the highest of standards for all of his students.

About the Author

Anne M. Beninghof, internationally recognized consultant and trainer, has more than 20 years of experience working with students with special needs, in a variety of public and private settings. She has been a special education teacher, faculty member of the University of Hartford and the University of Colorado, and has published several books and videos. Recently, Anne decided to follow her heart and return to the classroom, where she works part-time with teachers and students who are struggling with the learning process. In both her presenting and writing, Anne focuses on creative, practical solutions for more effectively including students with diverse learning needs in general education classrooms.

Contents

Introduction

It's a typical Tuesday in Mrs. McGough's third grade classroom. Of the 27 students on her class list, 24 are in attendance. Their ages range from 7.4 to 9.8, the youngest as the result of grade-skipping and a few of the oldest as a result of being retained. Nine of the 27 students are Hispanic, five are African American, one is Vietnamese, one is Native American, and 11 are Caucasian. Twelve students are from single-parent families, one lives with a grandparent, and four attended a different school at the beginning of the year. Boys outnumber girls, 17 to 10, and five of the boys have been identified as having special education needs.

There is nothing standard about children. They vary in innumerable ways—from external characteristics, such as shape, color, and size, to internal characteristics, such as life experience, learning style, and self-confidence. Just to walk into Mrs. McGough's classroom, or *any* classroom in the United States or Canada, is to know the truth of their individuality. Any teacher, with even a day's experience under his or her belt, knows the truth of this. Teachers witness how children attack math problems from different angles, ask surprising questions, and use phrases unique to their family's dialogue.

If we accept that children are unique in many ways, then our discussion of and planning for standards-based education must take this into account. This is the only way to achieve the goal of "success for all." Unfortunately, much of the discussion about standards has ignored students' individuality. As a growing number of people demand high standards and equal access for all, discussion about individualization has been shunted to the sidelines. State by state, there has been a rapid move to adopt a package of standards and to hold teachers and administrators accountable for their accomplishment, often without consideration of the unique needs of each classroom and school.

As this movement has progressed, the voices of concerned teachers have begun to be heard. In addition to calling for high standards for all, teachers are calling for instructional strategies and resources to make this dream a reality. They want to ensure that individual needs are met and believe that this will inevitably result in high achievement for all.

The mission of this book is to offer a wide variety of strategies that can be used to teach students with diverse learning needs. These strategies address many of the standards of learning, but also address the need for flexible, motivating, hands-on instruction. When you use these strategies to support your standards of learning, you will see, as other educators have, that your students can achieve high levels of learning.

Chapters 1, 2, and 3 provide a brief history of the standards-based education movement, current research findings, and a simple process to guide you in choosing strategies that match your students' needs.

Chapter 5 is replete with instructional strategies chosen for their versatility. Each strategy meets these criteria:

- ⟳ Free or inexpensive
- ⟳ Proven successful in scientific, action, or informal research
- ⟳ Relatively easy to implement
- ⟳ Applicable to numerous standards.

Commonly Used Terms

Benchmarks – a series of statements that indicate the best level of knowledge or skill that can be expected of students at a specific point in time. Often used synonymously with "standard"; occasionally used to indicate a subset of a broader standard.

Indicators – a series of small skills, usually listed sequentially, that when taken together form a broader body of knowledge or skills called a standard.

Standards – written statements that serve as a succinct description of what students are expected to know and be able to do at the completion of a given grade level.

Standards-based education – developing and implementing educational practices so that all students achieve a specified set of standards.

Chapter 5 provides an overview of each strategy, step-by-step implementation guidelines, and standards links. The links are examples of key standards that can be supported by the strategy. However, most strategies can be used to support *dozens* of standards across the content areas. Chapter 6 will help you make the most of each strategy. As you begin implementing the strategies, you will see how easily they generalize to support student learning.

History of the Standards Movement

It may seem as if the standards movement came out of nowhere, but in reality this movement has been building for years. It can be traced back to 1983, with the release of the report *A Nation at Risk* (National Commission on Excellence in Education). This federally funded review of the public education system of the United States concluded that the condition of schools was so poor as to "threaten our very future." In response to these words of warning, educators, legislators, parents, business owners, and other community members grew increasingly concerned.

In 1989, President George Bush convened a meeting of the nation's governors to address these concerns. This education summit resulted in the now famous *The National Education Goals Report*. This report outlined six key goals for the improvement of public education. In 1994 these goals were expanded by Congress to include two more. The eight goals are:

Goal 1: Ready to Learn

By the year 2000, all children in America will start school ready to learn.

Goal 2: School Completion

By the year 2000, the high school graduation rate will increase to at least 90%.

Goal 3: Student Achievement and Citizenship

By the year 2000, American students will leave grades 4, 8, and 12 having demonstrated competency in challenging subject matter, including language arts, mathematics, science, history, and geography; and every school in America will ensure that all students learn to use their minds well, so they may be prepared for responsible citizenship, further learning, and productive employment in our modern economy.

Goal 4: Teacher Education and Professional Development

By the year 2000, the nation's teaching force will have access to programs for the continued improvement of their professional skills and will have the opportunity to acquire the knowledge and skills needed to instruct and prepare all American students for the next century.

Goal 5: Mathematics and Science

By the year 2000, U.S. students will be first in the world in science and mathematics achievement.

Goal 6: Adult Literacy and Lifelong Learning

By the year 2000, every adult American will be literate and will possess the knowledge and skills necessary to compete in a global economy and exercise the rights and responsibilities of citizenship.

Goal 7: Safe, Disciplined, and Alcohol- and Drug-Free Schools

By the year 2000, every school in the United States will be free of drugs, violence, and the unauthorized presence of firearms and alcohol, and every school will offer a disciplined environment conducive to learning.

Goal 8: Parental Participation

By the year 2000, every school will promote partnerships that will increase parental involvement and participation in promoting social, emotional, and academic growth of children.

To assist in the achievement of these goals, in 1994 the U.S. Congress passed the Goals 2000: Educate America Act. This act provided funding to the states (with flow through to school districts) to develop and implement educational systems to directly achieve the eight goals.

Congress showed its support of the standards movement when they reauthorized the Elementary and Secondary Education Act in 1994. Title I of this act requires states to adopt challenging content standards (as promoted by Goals 2000) in order to receive Title I funding. Once the money was linked to high standards, the movement was quickly underway at the state level.

While this was taking place within the federal and state education agencies, professional education organizations (such as National Council of Teachers of Mathematics) were busy designing proposed national standards in their various content areas. Mathematics standards were the first to be developed on a large scale (1989), probably because of the very specific focus of Goal 5. By the mid-1990s standards had been proposed for most content areas, some of which have been updated more recently. (See Appendix A, *Proposed Standards from National Organizations* for specific sources.)

But when did the standards movement reach the classroom? This has varied dramatically from state to state, and even from district to district. In certain states, teachers have been directly involved with standards implementation since the early 1990s. In other states, teachers have only recently sensed the impact of standards in their classrooms. In general, the standards movement reaches the classroom level when a statewide competency test is instituted. As of 2001, three-fourths of the states have mandated that students pass statewide tests in order to graduate. Several of the remaining states are currently in the process of mandating this as well. Many states have also entered into a phase of test revisions based on their experiences. Test revisions typically include an increase of performance-based items and increased test accommodations available for students with disabilities.

Districts have also varied in the degree of support provided to teachers. Some districts provide teachers with extensive staff development regarding state and local standards. Their staff development includes general information, specific benchmark analysis, strategies for teaching to standards, test score analysis, and remediation techniques. Other districts have left teachers to flounder on their own.

As Elliott Eisner, a nationally recognized assessment expert, writes, "The current emphasis on standards will provide no panacea in education. Paying close attention to how we teach and building institutions that make it possible for teachers to continue to grow as professionals may be much more effective educationally than trying to determine through standard means whether or not our students measure up" (Eisner 1993). Many leaders in the field agree with Eisner that support for teachers is critical. Unfortunately, few schools have been able to quickly develop systems that ensure quality professional development for teachers (Miles and Guiney 2000). While schools struggle with developing systems, the next phase of the standards movement has taken hold—accountability.

States and districts, in response to public demand, have developed several layers of accountability related to standards. These layers go beyond student testing and include funding, job security, and school management. While accountability systems are essential to any major change effort, they are most effective when developed in a fair and thoughtful manner, with proper resources and supports in place. As with other phases of the standards movement, the accountability phase may need to go through several iterations before each state has an effective system. In the meantime, educators at the classroom level are under more pressure than ever to raise student achievement levels.

Where does the standards movement leave us now? Most educators are putting their energy into effective implementation of the standards. By varying instructional strategies and teaching methods to address the needs of diverse learners, we are sure to help students experience greater success. If teachers maintain a child-focus, it is likely that the accountability and test-taking issues will sort themselves out. We will look back on the standards-based education movement and realize that holding high expectations and using effective instructional strategies does indeed lead to achievement for all.

The Connection Between Instruction and Struggling Students

In 2000, President George W. Bush promised "No child will be left behind." If the standards-based education movement is going to fulfill this promise, then we must include all students. This means including students with mental retardation, as well as those with high IQs. This means including students who learn easily, as well as those with learning disabilities. *All* must mean *all*. However, some students pose a much greater challenge to teachers than others. Typically, these are the struggling students—the ones who take more time, need more help, or just don't seem to "get it." For some of these students, higher standards impose a "forbidding barrier," rather than an exciting challenge (Governor's Task Force on Readiness 1987).

We know from experience and research that many factors affect learning. Some factors, such as home environment and health, may be difficult to control. Luckily, other factors can be heavily influenced by classroom-level teaching decisions. Teachers can adjust pacing, instructional style, materials, and many other factors to promote optimal learning conditions. Of these many variables, one stands out as extremely critical to struggling students. The research on learning styles shows that struggling students often have learning preferences that differ from traditional school practices. By being familiar with this research, and making instruction decisions based on it, teachers can increase the likelihood of student success. Key learning style components include:

- ⟳ Time of day
- ⟳ Classroom structure
- ⟳ Lighting
- ⟳ Sound
- ⟳ Perceptual modalities.

Time of day

At-risk and struggling students tend to prefer instruction later in the day (Callan 1998; Dunn 1996). Unfortunately, most educators are "morning people" and tend to teach the most important subjects first thing in the morning. Many schools have rigid schedules that place literary blocks in the morning for all classes, every day. But research shows that this may not be best for students. Barron, Henderson, and Spurgeon (1994) conducted a study in which struggling students were given literacy instruction in the afternoon. The researchers found an overall increase in the reading scores of these students, as compared to those taught in the morning.

Classroom structure

Preference for informal seating, movement, and a variety of learning arrangements also characterize the typical student who is not performing well in school. In Dunn's studies (1996), students did best with teachers who were willing to accommodate these learning differences.

Lighting

Lighting can have a huge impact on our ability to learn. Researchers have found that learning takes place faster in natural lighting than in artificial lighting (Viadero 2000). Unfortunately, many special education students spend a significant portion of their day receiving individualized instruction in resource rooms, which are often interior rooms in the building without windows. In addition, research (Dunn 1996) suggests that these same students prefer dimmer lighting than the traditional overhead fluorescent lighting provides.

Sound

High levels of background noise can also interfere with learning. Students with attention difficulties often have difficulty distinguishing teacher speech from other classroom noise. They may miss hearing minor differences between words, and this may affect their reading, comprehension, and direction-following skills. Many students identified as disabled experience this type of fluctuating hearing loss (Anderson 2001).

Perceptual modalities

Research on the perceptual modalities (visual, auditory, tactile, and kinesthetic) provides some disturbing information. While the vast majority of instruction in schools is auditory and visual, the vast majority of students in special education, those who drop out from high school, and those considered to be at risk for school failure are primarily tactile and kinesthetic learners (Dunn 1996; Carbo, Dunn, and Dunn 1991). Therefore, there is a large discrepancy between how teachers tend to teach and how most of these students learn best.

If we want students to meet standards, then learning-style factors are important considerations. We must examine our teaching practices for ways to reach all learners. As Lois Easton, a leader in professional development, wrote in an editorial in *Education Week* (2000), "Achievement used to be a variable. Students performed variously well or poorly.... With achievement as a variable, other factors of schooling could be absolutes. Time and place, curriculum, learning styles and assessment techniques—all of these could be absolutes. ... But things are changing. ... in order to make achievement an absolute, everything that was in the old formula must become a variable. ... The refrain should be 'All students can achieve the standards if time, space, curriculum, learning style and assessment techniques are variables.'"

Many teachers have recognized the need to vary their instruction and have integrated thoughtfully chosen variety into their day-to-day practices. A major study, "How Teaching Matters: Bringing the Classroom Back into Discussions of Teacher Quality" (Wenglinsky 2000) examined teacher practices and their relationship to high performance of students. The study looked at nearly 15,000 scores of eighth-graders in the math and sciences portions of the National Assessment of Educational Progress (NAEP). The findings clearly show that students who performed ahead of their peers were taught by teachers who integrated hands-on learning, critical thinking, and frequent teacher-developed assessments into their lessons. Students whose teachers used hands-on learning tasks scored from 40 to 72 percent ahead of their peers. Unfortunately, the report says, too few teachers implement these practices in their teaching. This most adversely affects students who are already failing to reach the standards.

Another major study, using a meta-analysis, looked at hundreds of research projects related to instructional strategies (Marzano, Gaddy, and Dean 2000). During this analysis, the authors identified the nine most powerful instructional strategies for affecting student achievement. In order of highest benefit, they are:

1. Identifying similarities and differences
2. Summarizing and note-taking
3. Reinforcing effort and providing recognition
4. Homework and practice
5. Nonlinguistic representations
6. Cooperative learning
7. Setting goals and providing feedback
8. Generating and testing hypotheses
9. Activating prior knowledge.

While many of these strategies can be implemented through hands-on tasks, the fifth strategy directly describes the use of active instructional medium. The authors define "nonlinguistic representations" as the use of graphic organizers, pictures, visualization, concrete representations, and kinesthetic activity. The fact that this surfaces as one of the best instructional strategies will probably not surprise you if you work with students with disabilities.

9

From experience, you know that active, kinesthetic instructional tasks are often the most successful ways to keep students engaged and learning. Research also supports the use of manipulatives, multisensory materials, visual organizers, and physical involvement for students learning English as a second language (Gonzales 1995).

If this evidence is not a strong enough reason for making your instruction more diverse and hands-on, then perhaps Mara Sapon-Shevin's moral arguments for teaching acceptance of diversity (2001) will convince:

> Whole class instruction that demands identical student responses to the same material delivered in one format is consistent neither with our current understanding of student diversity nor with our changing models of teaching. We must ground our strategies of teaching in our understanding of students' multiple identities and communities. *By using diverse teaching strategies, teachers not only improve their chances of reaching every learner, but also model respect for diversity and help students understand that people are different and learn differently* (emphasis added).

Chapter 3

The Link Process for Developing Standards-Based Strategies

When teachers work with struggling students, time is of the essence. Because of this, we usually celebrate a quick solution to a learning problem. Although quick, effective solutions are a bonus, they are usually illusive. It is common for teachers to find a novel strategy that works for a few days before students lose interest. Or, teachers may embark upon an idea that a colleague raved about, only to find that it doesn't seem to help their own students at all. After awhile, the "quick fix" mentality becomes tiring, and teachers begin to lose hope of finding solutions.

Research and practice suggests that there is a better way. By taking the time to follow a proven problem-solving process, you can find successful interventions to match the needs of your learners (Polloway et al. 1996; Brimberry 1996; Nickols 1994; Kovaleski, Gickling, and Morrow 1999). In addition, by following a structured process, you can collect evidence of your intervention attempts and be prepared to respond to the call for accountability.

The challenge, however, is to find a process that is time efficient and realistic for today's demanding schools. To meet this challenge, I've developed the Link Process (*Figure 3.1*). This process is efficient and effective, yet simple. It will help you to focus on the steps necessary to develop strategies that support the standards of learning. Rather than offering a quick fix, it requires you to spend a few moments considering what you know about the learner and the standards. Then you can link to appropriate interventions based on this key information.

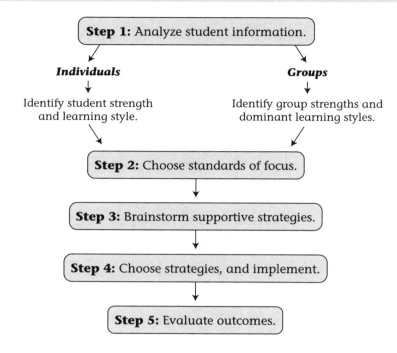

Figure 3.1: The five steps of the Link Process enable you to develop standards-based strategies that work.

Let's look at each step of the Link Process to see how it can work to bring about success for your struggling students. Follow along as we utilize the Link Process for Kengy, Zak, and Mavi—three struggling students—illustrated in *Figure 3.2*.

Introducing Kengy, Zak, and Mavi

Kengy – Seven-year-old Kengy enjoys first grade, but is becoming frustrated. His peers are beginning to read while he struggles with remembering letter sounds. He is aware of social cues and realizes he's not "getting it." Kengy's teacher, Ms. Kohn, wants to find some effective strategies before Kengy's motivation runs out.

Zak – Enthusiasm and energy make Zak a positive addition to his third grade class. However, his high energy also interferes with his attention span. Zak's comprehension of written material is well below grade level. His teacher, Mr. Bartley, knows that comprehension demands will increase significantly in fourth grade. How can he keep Zak focused and listening?

Mavi – Hard-working Mavi likes a quiet learning environment and concrete learning experiences. Fifth-grade mathematics poses huge challenges for her as the material becomes more and more abstract. Mavi's teacher, Ms. Archuleta, is looking for strategies that can help concrete learners, like Mavi, master a variety of abstract concepts.

The Link Process

Step 1: Analyze student information.

Almost every school in the United States and Canada uses some form of a standardized test to assess student learning. Over the last few years, many of these tests have been developed to link directly to state and national standards. In Colorado, for example, CTB/McGraw-Hill worked with local educators and the Colorado Department of Education to develop the Colorado Student Assessment Program (CSAP), a series of standardized tests based on the Colorado Content Standards. The scores provide schools with data on individual and group progress toward meeting the standards.

If tests are aligned with district content standards, then analysis of the test scores can provide educators with helpful information on areas of strength and weakness. As Ferrandino and Tirozzi (2001) state: "If we hope to raise the academic bar for all students by providing a challenging, quality curriculum, then we must test and fully assess students' comprehension and knowledge. We must know what they are learning and not learning."

Well-designed tests can provide some of the information teachers need. However, additional information about student learning must also be considered. The single snapshot provided by a standardized test does not yield thorough knowledge of a struggling student's learning. A more comprehensive

14

gathering of information is needed. As noted in *Education Week*, 29 November 2000, "Unless schools do a better job of collecting and analyzing the products of learning, teaching experts say, the drive to align classroom instruction with states' academic standards and testing programs will be incomplete."

What type of additional collection and analysis helps to complete the picture? The following sources yield important information:

- ➲ Anecdotal records from current and previous teachers
- ➲ Attendance records
- ➲ Behavioral observations
- ➲ Journal entries
- ➲ Language evaluations
- ➲ Learning style assessment
- ➲ Log of favorite book titles
- ➲ Portfolios
- ➲ Running records of oral reading
- ➲ Student and parent interviews
- ➲ Student work samples
- ➲ Teacher-made tests.

The more we know about a student from thoughtful data analysis, the more likely we will be able to forge a link between the area of need and the best strategy for the individual. Because the research on learning styles of struggling students is compelling, this may be one of the most critical pieces of information to collect. Although there are several comprehensive, well-validated, learning style assessment tools (Dunn, Dunn, and Price 1994; Carbo 1994; McCarthy 1993), you will probably find it easiest to use your own observation skills. Researchers have found that classroom teachers are highly accurate in determining a student's perceptual modality preferences simply through observation (Dunn, Dunn, and Price 1977).

Learning style information serves as a stepping-stone for developing and implementing strategies aimed at improving student achievement. By taking a few moments to consider learning style information at the beginning of the problem-solving process, you will save time and energy in the long run. Most importantly, your strategies will be directly linked to students' individual needs, making your approach more effective!

Reproducible 3.1, *Student Learning Style Observation* (Beninghof 1998), in the Reproducibles section will guide you in collecting and categorizing observational data for each of the four perceptual modalities (visual, auditory, tactile, and kinesthetic). Simply check off the behaviors you frequently see a student demonstrating in your classroom. The pattern of check marks helps you determine the student's learning style. As you collect this critical data, you can summarize it for future reflection using Reproducible 3.2, *Student Information Form*.

You can see how Kengy's, Zak's, and Mavi's teachers begin the Link Process with the *Student Information Form*, in *Figures 3.3, 3.4,* and *3.5* using information they collected with the *Student Information Form*.

Figure 3.3: Ms. Kohn uses Reproducible 3.2, *Student Information Form* to collect information about Kengy.

Student Information Form

Student Name _Kengy_ _____ Grade _1_ Date _____

Teacher _Ms. Kohn_ _____ _____

Gather and analyze information about the student. Be sure to include student strengths and needs.

Standardized Test Scores

Not available in first grade

Classroom Assessments (e.g., informal reading inventories, work samples, teacher-made tests)

Informal Reading Inventory (IRI):
- *Word identification 60%*
- *Comprehension 50% (when reading along with teacher 100%)*
- *Kindergarten checklist: Names 22/26 letters, Sounds for 15/26 letters*
- *Knows first 25 sight words on Fry list*

Anecdotal Information

Kengy enjoys books and will choose them for his free time activity. He is showing good book sense—orientation, attention to pictures, awareness of title. His sight vocabulary is strong relative to his other skills and to his peers. Memory for sound/symbol connection is weak. He seems to understand the connections during small group or one-on-one instruction, but then forgets them quickly. Kengy uses picture clues and semantics to make good guesses of unknown words. Good artist.

Learning Styles

Appears stronger visually than auditorily. Very social and looks to peers for cues. May be more global than analytic.

© 2003 Sopris West. All rights reserved. (800) 547-6747, item number 154MEET.

Figure 3.4: Mr. Bartley uses Reproducible 3.2, *Student Information Form* to collect information about Zak.

Student Information Form

Student Name ___Zak_____ Grade __3__ Date _____

Teacher ___Mr. Bartley_____

Gather and analyze information about the student. Be sure to include student strengths and needs.

Standardized Test Scores

State Assessment Program (SAP):
Partially proficient
Item analysis shows that Zak's incorrect items were linked to the following skills:

- *Finding the sequence of events in a story*
- *Finding or recalling events in a story*

- *Determining the main idea of a story*
- *Finding or recalling details in a story*
- *Determining the main idea in nonfiction*
- *Drawing conclusions and inferences*

Classroom Assessments (e.g., informal reading inventories, work samples, teacher-made tests)

Informal Reading Inventory (IRI):
- *Word identification 93%*
- *Fluency 28 words per minute (2nd grade equivalent)*
- *Comprehension 65%*

Anecdotal Information

Zak is active during group reading exercises, frequently wiggling or out of his seat. He does not appear to follow along. When reading aloud, Zak reads very slowly but with a good deal of accuracy. He shows very little inflection when reading. Zak has a difficult time retelling any part of what he has read. Silent reading results are similar to oral reading. Zak does use picture clues to aid his comprehension.

Learning Styles

Preferences for kinesthetic learning, informal seating; probably a global thinker. Loves music and is frequently singing.

© 2003 Sopris West. All rights reserved. (800) 547-6747, item number 154MEET.

Student Information Form

Student Name __Mavi__ ____ Grade __5__ Date _____

Teacher __Ms. Archuleta__ _____

Gather and analyze information about the student. Be sure to include student strengths and needs.

Standardized Test Scores

State Assessment Program (SAP):
Partially proficient

Item analysis shows that Mavi's incorrect items were linked to the following skills:
– Knows the difference between pertinent and irrelevant information when solving problems
– Uses trial and error and the process of elimination to solve problems

– Understands the basic meaning of place value
– Understands the relative magnitude and relationships among whole numbers, fractions, decimals, and mixed numbers
– Uses specific strategies to estimate computations and to check the reasonableness of computational results

Classroom Assessments (e.g., informal reading inventories, work samples, teacher-made tests)

Simple computation is on grade level.

Fraction test 65%

Decimal test 58%

Word problems 60% average

Math interview: Mavi cannot usually explain how she arrived at an answer or why she chose a specific approach. When dissecting a word problem, Mavi does not identify key information before trying to solve the problem.

Anecdotal Information

Mavi tries very hard in math, determined to match her peers. However, she doesn't seem to understand more abstract or complicated math problems. When we try to talk through process, she loses attention and comprehension. This is true in the writing process, as well, but she is managing to stay on grade level in writing. She does best with very concrete information. Her previous teachers report that she learned her basic computation with the help of manipulatives.

Learning Styles

Preferences for tactile, concrete approaches. Likes a quiet, distraction-free setting.

© 2003 Sopris West. All rights reserved. (800) 547-6747, item number 154MEET.

Step 2: Choose standards of focus.

After analyzing student information, you may find many areas in which improvement is desired. Even though you will want to address all the areas, it is important to choose just one or two standards for your initial focus. Often, teachers get caught up in trying to do it all at once and don't experience much success. If you focus your efforts, you will be more successful in the long run (Calhoun 1999; Beninghof and Singer 1995; Nickols 1994).

Whether you are choosing a standard of focus for a group of students or an individual, there are several essential questions to consider. You may wish

18

to reflect on these by yourself, or ask a few trusted colleagues to assist you. By asking and answering the following six questions, you clarify your thinking and are better able to choose which standards deserve your immediate attention.

1. Does the school/district have a curricular area of greatest concern at this time, e.g., writing or science?

2. Are other initiatives underway in the school/district that could be supported by my choices?

3. Considering other efforts underway in the school/district, is my effort likely to be redundant?

4. Is there a significant discrepancy between two or more skill or subject areas?

5. Is there a specific standard or learning objective that must be addressed before the student(s) can be promoted?

6. Is the most important goal to change student test scores from "no progress" to "partially proficient," from "partially proficient" to "proficient," or from "proficient" to "advanced"? (Some districts target a specific student group as their highest priority.)

Once you complete your analysis of student information and choose standards of focus, use Reproducible 3.3, *Standards-Based Strategies for Individual Students* and Reproducible 3.4, *Standards-Based Strategies for Groups* to record your decisions.

Summarize what you know about the learner's strengths, needs, and learning styles in the boxes at the top of the form. Next, write down the content area and chosen standard(s) of focus.

You can look at the *Standards-Based Strategies for Individual Students* forms for Kengy, Zak, and Mavi (*Figures 3.6, 3.7,* and *3.8*), beginning on the next page, to see how their teachers summarized student information and chose standards that require immediate focus. They are now halfway through the Link Process and on their way to finding instructional solutions!

Figure 3.6: Ms. Kohn uses Reproducible 3.3, *Standards-Based Strategies for Individual Students* to focus her problem-solving.

Standards-Based Strategies for Individual Students

Student Name __Kengy__   Grade __1__   Date __2/27__

Teacher(s) __Ms. Kohn__

Student Information

Areas of Strength		Learning Styles	Areas of Need
Uses picture clues	Social	Visual	Sound/symbol connection
Artistic	Good book sense	Social	Memory
Sight vocabulary	Uses clues	Global thinker	
		Spatial	

Standards of Focus

Content Area __Reading__   Content Area _____

Standard	Standard
Uses the general skills and strategies of the reading process - Uses basic elements of phonetic analysis to decode unknown words	
Supportive Strategies	**Supportive Strategies**

Evaluation Plan

Process	Date(s)	Person(s) Responsible

© 2003 Sopris West. All rights reserved. (800) 547-6747, item number 154MEET.

Standards-Based Strategies for Individual Students

Student Name _Zak_   Grade 3   Date _10/15_

Teacher(s) _Mr. Bartley_

Student Information

Areas of Strength	Learning Styles	Areas of Need
Word attack Likes books	Tactile and kinesthetic	Comprehension Fluency Retelling Attention span Details

Standards of Focus

Content Area _Reading_   Content Area _Reading_

Standard	Standard

Uses reading skills and strategies to understand and interpret a variety of literary texts
  – Knows setting, main characters, main events, sequence and problems in stories
  – Makes simple inferences
  – Knows the main ideas or theme of a story
	Uses the general skills and strategies of the reading process
	  – Reads aloud familiar stories, poems, and passages with fluency and expression

Supportive Strategies	Supportive Strategies

Evaluation Plan

Process	Date(s)	Person(s) Responsible

© 2003 Sopris West. All rights reserved. (800) 547-6747, item number 154MEET.

Figure 3.8: Ms. Archuleta uses Reproducible 3.2, *Standards-Based Strategies for Individual Students* to focus her problem-solving.

Standards-Based Strategies for Individual Students

Student Name Mavi   Grade 5   Date 11/14 ____

Teacher(s) Ms. Archuleta   _____

Student Information

Areas of Strength	Learning Styles	Areas of Need
Simple computation	Concrete	Word problems Decimals
Good effort	Tactile	Math processes
Concrete information	Prefers quiet	Place value
		Fractions

Standards of Focus

Content Area   Math   Content Area   Math

Standard	Standard
Use numbers and number relationships in problem-solving situations to communicate reasoning – Discovers fractional meanings – Names and compares common fractions and decimals and determine relationships	Develops number sense and uses numbers and number relationships in problem-solving situations to communicate the reasoning used in solving these problems – Uses math vocabulary to develop greater understanding about number relationships – Determines when patterns and relationships are logical and lead to reasonable conclusions
Supportive Strategies	Supportive Strategies

Evaluation Plan

Process	Date(s)	Person(s) Responsible

© 2003 Sopris West. All rights reserved. (800) 547-6747, item number 154MEET.

Reproducible 3.3

Meeting Standards

137

21

Meeting Standards

Step 3: Brainstorm supportive strategies.

With all the good information you've collected and a clear focus, you are well-prepared to brainstorm supportive strategies. Although the vast majority of educators have brainstormed many times in their lives, few have ever brainstormed according to the original rules of brainstorming.

Brainstorming was originally developed as a structured process for problem-solving by Alex Osborne (1963). While he was running his own business, Osborne became concerned that his employees lacked the ability to be creative. After doing some research, he determined that the greatest inhibitor of creative thought was the fear of judgment or ridicule. In response, Osborne developed a process that would encourage creativity by restricting judgment. He developed several rules for the process he named *brainstorming*, the most important rule being "no judgment." By this Osborne didn't just mean no criticism. His rule was intended to eliminate both *positive* and *negative* judgment. To emphasize his point, Osborne banned comments such as "I've tried that before" and "Good idea, but...." He found that these comments, while not typically viewed as negative judgments, decreased the flow of creative ideas as severely as more direct criticism.

Osborne's second brainstorming rule was to shoot for a large quantity of ideas, rather than worry about quality. Why? Because if you worry about quality, then you prejudge your own ideas. Prejudgment decreases innovation and limits possible solutions. Worried about others' reactions, people keep their ideas to themselves. When this happens, the team loses valuable options and ends up with only a short list of ideas. Osborne encouraged teams to develop longer and longer lists each time they brainstormed.

Most teachers who participate in group problem-solving find that their ideas are greeted with all kinds of reactions. Unfortunately, as Osborne found, some of these reactions decrease the group's ability to creatively solve the problem before them. With the increased pressure to reach standards, and the increase of accountability mechanisms, educators must find a process that produces creative solutions.

As you begin to develop standards-based strategies, remember to go easy on the judgments. Create long lists of ideas from which to pick and choose the best.

You can look at the long brainstormed lists of Kengy's, Zak's, and Mavi's teachers in *Figures 3.9*, *3.10*, and *3.11*, beginning on the next page.

Brainstorm for Kengy

- *Listen to books on tape*
- *Read with an older reading buddy*
- *Feedback pipe*
- *Sound drawings*
- *Look in a mirror while making sounds*
- *Rhyming books*
- *Make up chants about sounds/letters*
- *Tape self on tape recorder*
- *Alphabet strip for his bedroom*
- *Hop-step mat with letters*
- *Highlighter tape for letters/sounds*
- *Letter of the day or week*
- *Homework – find as many objects that start with …*
- *Jump up every time you hear …*
- *Raise your hand if you see the letter …*
- *Make a list of words that start with the same sound*
- *Make a picture book of words that start with the same sound*
- *I Spy Quilt*
- *I Spy books*
- *Triple vocal rehearse of words*
- *Conversation books with a focus letter*
- *Teacher's helper to point out letters/sounds*
- *Grabber for the overhead*

Figure 3.10: Mr. Bartley's brainstorm list of possible strategies for Zak.

Brainstorm for Zak

- Story element fortune teller
- Retelling trios
- Highlighting tape to color-code story elements
- "Chunking" strategy
- Color strips
- Distraction-free reading area
- Break after each paragraph to summarize
- Question cubes strategy after the story
- Hop-step mat with first, next, last
- Radio review – summary into tape recorder
- Listen to self read and summarize on recorder
- Use graphic organizer to catch info along the way
- Beat your score – summarize in ten words or less
- Circle story elements with Wikki Stix
- Read along with fluent reader
- Story element question cards – use with partner
- Visualize with eyes closed after reading a segment
- Draw a quick summary of each section
- Erasable highlighters to highlight elements
- Make puzzle pieces of story
- Spinner of story elements – spin and tell
- Sticky notes while reading
- Small flashlight for reading along

Brainstorm for Mavi
- *Fact flipper strategy*
- *Draw math process pictures*
- *Cue card on desk of process*
- *Use of math manipulatives*
- *Hop-step mat to follow process*
- *Dice games strategy*
- *Playing cards*
- *Wikki Stix to make connections*
- *Game piece to move through steps of process*
- *Graphic organizers for math processes*
- *Clear plastic page covers and transparency markers*
- *White board to show work*
- *Quiet work space*
- *Computer software*
- *Make up word problems with parent*
- *Teacher's helper to make up word problems*
- *Work at standing work station*
- *Use color cubes to build concrete representations*
- *Act out word problems*
- *Use small toys at home to work out math problems*
- *Use coins to practice number relationships*
- *Stepping stones strategy*
- *Older student to tutor*

Step 4: Choose strategies, and implement.

Once you have a brainstormed list, choose a few strategies to try. Making choices may be easy; you may see one idea you love and go with it. But sometimes it is difficult to determine which strategy is best. The following questions can help guide your decision-making process:

1. How does this idea fit with my philosophy and values?
2. What is the quickest solution?
3. What is the most long-lasting solution?
4. Which idea is the easiest to implement?
5. How does this idea fit with school policies?
6. Which solution fits best with my teaching style?
7. Is the time right for this solution?
8. What if this idea fails? What could go wrong?
9. What is the least intrusive solution? To whom?
10. Can more than one solution be attempted at the same time?

Step 5: Evaluate outcomes.

Develop a simple evaluation plan to help you judge the student's success. Implement your strategy for a few weeks before evaluating its effectiveness, but don't let too much time pass before checking out your strategy. You want to be sure you are headed in the right direction. Most teachers find that three to five weeks is about right.

What type of evaluation is necessary? Simple, informal assessments are usually best. If these show that sufficient progress is being made, continue with the strategies for as long as they are helpful. On the other hand, if informal measures show a lack of progress, choose some alternate strategies, intensify the supports, or perform a more comprehensive evaluation.

Now let's see which strategies were chosen for Kengy, Zak, and Mavi, and how their teachers plan to evaluate progress. (See *Figures 3.12*, *3.13*, and *3.14*, beginning on the following page.)

Standards-Based Strategies for Individual Students

Student Name *Kengy*   Grade *1*   Date *2/27*

Teacher(s) *Ms. Kohn*

Student Information

Areas of Strength		Learning Styles	Areas of Need
Uses picture clues	*Social*	*Visual*	*Sound/symbol connection*
Artistic	*Good book sense*	*Social*	*Memory*
Sight vocabulary	*Uses clues*	*Global thinker*	
		Spatial	

Standards of Focus

Content Area *Reading*   Content Area _____

Standard	Standard
Uses the general skills and strategies of the reading process *- Uses basic elements of phonetic analysis to decode unknown words*	
Supportive Strategies	**Supportive Strategies**
Feedback pipe *Sound drawings* *Chants and rhymes* *Alphabet strip for his bedroom* *Partner reading*	

Evaluation Plan

Process	Date(s)	Person(s) Responsible
Kindergarten checklist retake	*3/28*	*Ms. Lucas*
Informal Reading Inventory	*3/30*	*Ms. Kohn*

© 2003 Sopris West. All rights reserved. (800) 547-6747, item number 154MEET.

Figure 3.13: Mr. Bartley adds supportive strategies and an evaluation plan to Zak's *Standards-Based Strategies for Individual Students* (Reproducible 3.3).

Standards-Based Strategies for Individual Students

Student Name _Zak_   Grade 3   Date _10/15_ ___

Teacher(s) _Mr. Bartley_

Student Information

Areas of Strength	Learning Styles	Areas of Need
Word attack Likes books	Tactile and kinesthetic	Comprehension Fluency Retelling Attention span Details

Standards of Focus

Content Area _Reading_   Content Area _Reading_

Standard	Standard

Uses reading skills and strategies to understand and interpret a variety of literary texts
  – Knows setting, main characters, main events, sequence and problems in stories
  – Makes simple inferences
  – Knows the main ideas or theme of a story
	Uses the general skills and strategies of the reading process
	  – Reads aloud familiar stories, poems, and passages with fluency and expression

Supportive Strategies
  – Highlighting tape to color-code story elements
  – Hop-step mat "First, Next, Last"
  – Graphic organizer to fill in after finishing the story Supportive Strategies
	Supportive Strategies
	  – Teach "chunking"
	  – Listen to self on tape recorder
	  – Read along with fluent reader (in person or on tape)
	  – Stop and self-check

Evaluation Plan

Process	Date(s)	Person(s) Responsible

Follow-up Informal Reading Inventories
  – Fluency check
  – Comprehension questions
	11/1, 12/1	Mr. Bartley

© 2003 Sopris West. All rights reserved. (800) 547-6747, item number 154MEET.

28

Standards-Based Strategies for Individual Students

Student Name __Mavi__   Grade _5_   Date _11/14_ ____

Teacher(s) _Ms. Archuleta_ ____

Student Information

Areas of Strength	Learning Styles	Areas of Need
Simple computation Good effort Concrete information	Concrete Tactile Prefers quiet	Word problems Decimals Math processes Place value Fractions

Standards of Focus

Content Area _Math_   Content Area _Math_

Standard	Standard
Use numbers and number relationships in problem-solving situations to communicate reasoning – Discovers fractional meanings – Names and compares common fractions and decimals and determine relationships	Develop number sense and use numbers and number relationships in problem-solving situations to communicate the reasoning used in solving these problems – Uses math vocabulary to develop greater understanding about number relationships – Determines when patterns and relationships are logical and lead to reasonable conclusions
Supportive Strategies – Use of manipulatives – Computer software – Fact flipper	Supportive Strategies – Graphic organizers for math processes – Wikki Stix to make connections – Refrigerator magnets (teacher made)

Evaluation Plan

Process	Date(s)	Person(s) Responsible
Fraction and decimal tests – retake	12/20, 1/20	Ms. Archuleta
Word problem interview	1/30	Mr. Santos

© 2003 Sopris West. All rights reserved. (800) 547-6747, item number 154MEET.

Reproducible 3.3

137

Meeting Standards

29

Adapting the Link Process for Group Instruction

Individualized instruction has wonderful benefits for students, but group instruction is a necessary way of life in public schools. Even in a classroom with only 18 students, it is difficult to continuously offer specific instruction for each student. Go from that classroom to one down the hall with 28 students, and the task becomes impossible. Therefore, supportive strategies that work for groups of learners must be a part of your repertoire.

In addition to the prevalence of group instruction, there is another reason to develop group strategies: Groups of learners often share gaps in learning. For example, if the local curriculum is not completely aligned with the state's standards and assessment program, it is likely that test scores will show a large number of students as less proficient in a specific skill area. Let's say that your district math curriculum does not introduce *estimation* until the fourth grade, but the state standards and assessments program include *estimation* for third-graders. It is likely that a significant number of your third-graders will receive "partially proficient" or "not proficient" scores in *estimation*.

Sometimes group gaps are the result of teacher skill deficits or instructional emphasis. If last year's teacher was not a strong teacher of writing or emphasized "voice" more than "organization," students as a group may need supportive teaching strategies to help them organize their writing.

The approach to developing strategies for groups is the same as for individual students—except for two differences. The first difference is that groups need to be looked at as a whole; therefore, you need to develop a group learning profile. With a portrait of the entire group, you can choose strategies to match group needs. Your group profile can be based on standardized test scores, teacher-made tests, anecdotal records, etc. However, a key component of a group profile is information on learning styles. You can gather this information through formal learning style assessments or informal observations of individual students using Reproducible 3.1, *Student Learning Style Observation*. Once you collect information for each student in the group, you can collate it with Reproducible 3.5, *Group Learning Style Profile*.

The second difference between the process for individuals versus groups is that, with groups, it is critical to choose strategies with "treatment acceptability" (Polloway et al. 1996). That is, the strategies you choose need to be ones you can implement easily in a large group and general education setting. Strategies that do not meet this criterion are often not fully implemented, and therefore do not lead to student growth.

Because the Link Process for groups varies a bit from the process for individuals, a slightly different form is used. Reproducible 3.4, *Standards-Based Strategies for Groups*, provides a format for capturing and summarizing key information about your class. As with the process for individuals, be sure to summarize strengths, needs, and learning styles. Based on this information, choose standards of focus, brainstorm strategies, and develop an evaluation plan. *Figure 3.15* shows a group profile for Mrs. McGough's class. *Figure 3.16* shows how she followed the Link Process to develop supportive strategies.

Figure 3.15: Mrs. McGough's class profile.

Group Learning Style Profile

Group _____   _____

Teacher __Mrs. McGough_____   _____   Date __9/26_____

Write the names of students in the quadrant which most represents their dominant learning style.

Visual

T.J.
Brian
Sean
Inez
Grace
Brianna
Lucy
Guillermo
Steve
Jason

Auditory

Kyle
Charie
Tamika

Tactile

J.J.
Huong
Lenny
Manuel
Chandra
Tracy
Isidor

Kinesthetic

Eddie
Ricardo
Nathan
Olivia
Janelle
Terrell
Scotty

© 2003 Sopris West. All rights reserved. (800) 547-6747, item number 154MEET.

Meeting Standards

32

Reproducible 3.4

Meeting Standards

138

Standards-Based Strategies for Groups

Group _____   _____

Teacher(s) _Mrs. McGough_ _____   _____ Grade _3_____ Date _1/19_____

Group Information

Group Strengths	Group Learning Style		Group Needs
Predictions	V 10	A 3	Retelling
Connecting to prior learning	T 7	K 7	Story elements
Questioning			

Standards of Focus

Area _Reading_ _____   __ Area _____

Standard	Standard
Knows how literary elements can be used to make sense of narrative text	

Supportive Strategies	Supportive Strategies
- Color-coding with pencils - Graphic organizers - Highlighter Tape for story elements - Story element fortune tellers - Color-coded cubes to build story parts	

Evaluation Plan

Process	Date(s)	Person(s) Responsible
Retelling rubric – randomly selected students	2/28	Mrs. McGough

© 2003 Sopris West. All rights reserved. (800) 547-6747, item number 154MEET.

Chapter 4

The Connection Between Home and School

When the fitness craze hit the United States in the 1990s, many people trained for triathlon races (swimming, biking, and running). Some decided to compete in all three events by themselves, others recognized the advantages of teaming up. Teams had a clear edge. They were able to take advantage of individual expertise, share the work load, and support each other with encouragement. Ultimately the teams completed the events faster than individual competitors.

By teaming up with parents (and students!) you can make better use of available resources. In the race to achieve high standards for students within a reasonable time frame, you will have clear advantages if you partner with others, rather than go it alone. Families are an incredibly important resource. They affect their children's growth in almost every moment outside of school. All the choices parents make—which books to check out at the library, how much television viewing to allow, where homework gets done—affect learning. If you do not partner with parents, you are much less likely to achieve your goals.

Most parents have a strong desire to help their children succeed in school. However, many parents lack the knowledge of how to be most helpful. They don't know what to do when their children struggle with homework, can't master their math facts, or continue to confuse a "b" with a "d". Frustration can quickly build for parents, teachers, and worst of all, for students.

What is the solution? Perhaps it starts with the recognition that schools must give parents more information about effective instructional techniques. As Rick DuFour writes in an article in the *Journal of Staff Development* (2000), "Schools must give parents some direction about how to be most helpful. When schools present parents with an explanation of the skills children are to learn, along with specific strategies that enable a mother or father to participate in their child's development of those skills, everyone benefits."

Schools are providing information in many ways. Some districts offer parent training, others have resource libraries. Home visits and evening meetings provide forums for sharing ideas. These can be effective, but many times simple approaches work best for busy parents (and busy teachers, too!). Reproducible 4.1, *Standards-Based Home Strategies* will help you provide parents with specific information about the standards with which their children are struggling. You can use it to suggest specific activities parents can do to help their children meet standards. This will be most effective when activities are matched to students' learning styles. By providing information that is specific to their children, rather than generic ideas, parents will be more motivated to participate and more effective in their efforts.

After you identify a student's learning style and the specific standard of focus, completing Reproducible 4.1, *Standards-Based Home Strategies* is easy. First, reword the standard of focus from Reproducible 3.3, *Standards-Based Strategies for Individual Students* in parent-friendly language. Help the parent(s) understand the specific nature of the child's struggle. This will facilitate future communication about the problem. Second, describe simple strategies that the parent(s) may use at home to help the child. By listing ideas specific to both the standard and the unique learning style of the child, you increase the likelihood that the parent(s) will utilize the ideas and be effective.

> "These forms of (parent) involvement do not happen by accident or even by invitation. They happen by explicit strategic intervention."
>
> —Dr. Michael Fullen, Dean of Education, University of Toronto

Although it is best to discuss Reproducible 4.1 with parents in person, it may not always be possible to find face-to-face time. If you mail the form or send it home with the student, include a cover letter to further explain your goals. An example of a cover letter appears in *Figure 4.1*.

As you look at the home strategies for Kengy, Zak, and Mavi, in *Figures 4.2*, *4.3*, and *4.4* on the following pages, notice the clear wording of the standards. These teachers avoided using educational jargon. Also notice the suggested activities. They have chosen simple ideas that blend easily into busy family life. (Several of these strategies are described in detail in Chapter 5.)

Central Elementary School

Dear Parent,

At Central Elementary School we are working hard to improve student skills in all areas. Our teachers and staff are focusing instruction on the Standards for Learning suggested by our State Department of Education and national organizations. Our goal is for all children to accomplish their grade level standards by the end of the year. Your child has been having difficulty in one or more of the areas identified by these Standards for Learning.

We have been using a variety of instructional strategies to improve your child's skills in these areas. We know that you would also like to help your child succeed. For that reason, we are sending home a list of simple ideas that you can use when working with your child on homework, or when you are just spending time relaxing with your child. These ideas have been specifically selected to match your child's learning style.

Figure 4.2: Ms. Kohn's home strategies for Kengy.

Standards-Based Home Strategies

Student Name _Kengy_   Grade _1_   Date _2/27_

Teacher(s) _Ms. Kohn_   _____

Standard	Things to try at home
Your child is struggling with these standards in school.	You may want to try these things at home to help your child. Please contact your child's teacher if you have any questions.
Reading *Using a variety of strategies to figure out unfamiliar words*	– *Use a magazine or newspaper article to look at pictures. Have your child name the picture and guess what letter it starts or ends with.* – *Play the rhyming game. Say a word and ask your child to think of a word that rhymes with it. Take turns.* – *Use Wikki Stix (attached) to write simple words. Talk about the sounds in the words.* – *Form words with magnetic letters, Scrabble tiles, or letters written on index cards.*

© 2003 Sopris West. All rights reserved. (800) 547-6747, item number 154MEET.

Reproducible 4.1

140

36

Figure 4.3: Mr. Bartley's home strategies for Zak.

Standards-Based Home Strategies

Student Name _Zak_____   Grade _3_____   Date _10/15_____

Teacher(s) _Mr. Bartley_____   _____

Standard	**Things to try at home**
Your child is struggling with these standards in school.	You may want to try these things at home to help your child. Please contact your child's teacher if you have any questions.
Reading *Using a variety of strategies to understand what he is reading. Knowing the main idea of the story, the characters, and other important information.*	– *After your child has finished reading, ask him to tell you all about the story.* – *Have your child place a sticky note on each page. When he finishes the page, tell him to write a few words on the sticky note to tell about what he read.* – *Have your child draw a picture of what he read.* – *Use Highlighter Tape (attached) to have your child highlight information about the characters in the story.*
Reading *Reading aloud smoothly and with expression*	– *Ask your child to read a story into a tape recorder. Then have him listen to himself.* – *Read a sentence to your child, using lots of expression. Then ask him to read the same sentence, just like you did.* – *Read a paragraph to your child. Ask him to act it out while you read it a second time. Then ask him to read it with lots of expression.*

© 2003 Sopris West. All rights reserved. (800) 547-6747, item number 154MEET.

Standards-Based Home Strategies

Student Name ___Mavi_____ Grade _5_____ Date _11/14_____

Teacher(s) __Ms. Archuleta_____

Standard	Things to try at home
Your child is struggling with these standards in school.	You may want to try these things at home to help your child. Please contact your child's teacher if you have any questions.
Math *Understanding fractions and using them to solve real problems*	– Cut food into equal pieces and talk about the fractions you can make. – Ask her to divide her books into equal piles, then change them into a different number of piles. Talk about the fractions that result. – Use pennies, nickels, and dimes to talk about fractions. Have her sort and wrap money from a spare change jar and discuss.
Math *Explaining how to solve math problems*	– When cooking, talk about how to measure ingredients and how to change the recipe if you need to serve more people. – Play the "Name that Number" card game she learned in school. Have her explain her solutions to you. – Ask her to create simple math word problems that a younger child can solve. – Make an index card that reminds her what steps to take when working on multiplying decimals.

© 2003 Sopris West. All rights reserved. (800) 547-6747, item number 154MEET.

Supportive Strategies

Good teachers are idea collectors. Everywhere they go they look for simple, effective teaching ideas to use in their classrooms. They find them in expected and unexpected places—at the grocery store, at the recycling center, or on television. Once they find a "keeper," they store it for future use, in their heads, notebooks, or perhaps in computer files.

Over the years, I have become an idea collector, too. I seek out sensible, creative ideas from my everyday travels, from my work with students, and from my travels to classrooms around the U.S. As this journey has progressed, I have narrowed my search to ideas that are directly supportive of the standards being held out for our students. In narrowing my focus, I have discovered that high-quality instruction inevitably leads to success with standards.

The strategies in this chapter can be used to support the standards, but will also support the differentiation that is so needed for today's diverse learners.

Because research shows that most struggling students are tactile and kinesthetic learners, the vast majority of the strategies I have selected are "hands on." They are effective, easy ways to make instruction more interactive and engaging.

> The teachers have struggled to meet their first obligation—to ensure that a standards-based teaching practice is not in conflict with best teaching practice. Once the teachers aligned standards with high-quality instruction, differentiation followed naturally."
>
> —Dr. Carol Ann Tomlinson, educational leader, University of Virginia

Each strategy is presented in the following format:

Standards Links

At the beginning of each strategy, several academic standards are listed that are taken from state and national standards banks (also see Appendix A, *Proposed Standards from National Organizations*). The wording may not match your district's standards exactly, but the content is common to all schools. The strategy is directly applicable to the standards listed. Lifelong learning standards, or access skills (see Appendix B, *Access Skills*), are included in the standards links. Although these are not the focus of this book, access skills are essential to academic success. They are denoted with the icon:

Use Appendix C, *Linking Strategies to Subject Areas*, to find strategies linked to a specific content area. In addition to the suggested standards links, many other standards can be met using the strategies in this chapter. Be creative in using each strategy to meet standards of particular concern to you. Chapter 6, *Making the Most of Each Strategy*, provides ideas for generalizing and adapting.

Overview

Under this heading you will find a brief description of the strategy. A quick read will give you a sense of what the strategy can do for you and your students.

What to Do

Here's the best part: a step-by-step explanation of how to put this strategy to work in your classroom. Simple, yet comprehensive, this information will give you what you need to implement the strategy successfully.

Consider

Looking for more ideas? Here you will find variations and adaptations to help you make the most of a strategy. In addition, strategies can often be tweaked to support lifelong learning skills (like reducing those off-task behaviors!). Ideas in this section that support lifelong learning are also marked with a so you can quickly locate them.

Notes

This section allows you to write in your own adaptations and uses of the strategy.

Practicing Facts With Larry's "Laptop"

Standards Links

Mathematics: The student will recall basic addition facts, sums to 10 or less, and the corresponding subtraction facts.

Writing: The student will write to communicate ideas, using correct spelling for frequently used words.

Technology: The student will know the characteristics and uses of computer hardware and operating systems.

Overview

Larry's "laptop" is a simulated computer keyboard that students use to practice spelling words or math facts. By typing on the "laptop," students receive tactile input. This strategy simultaneously reinforces knowledge of the computer keyboard.

What to Do

1. Obtain a manila or colored file folder for each student.

2. On the outside of the folder, have the student write his/her name.

3. On the inside of the folder, glue a copy of Reproducible 5.1, *Larry's "Laptop" Keyboard.*

4. Laminate the folder for long-lasting use.

5. Ask students to take out their "laptops" and practice their spelling words or math facts by moving their fingers across the keys, as if they were typing on a keyboard.

Consider

- ⊃ Adapt this strategy for students with poor fine motor skills by eliminating function keys and enlarging the keyboard.

- ⊃ To add tactile or visual cues, outline each key with glue or craft paint.

Notes

Active Reading Using Highlighter Tape

Standards Links

Reading: The student will demonstrate comprehension of a variety of literary forms, including fiction, nonfiction, and poetry.

Social Studies: The student will develop historical analysis skills, including identifying, analyzing, and making generalizations using primary sources.

Science: The student will plan and conduct investigations in which unexpected or unusual quantitative data are recognized.

Overview

With Highlighter Tape (a restickable adhesive) students highlight elements in texts in various colors, without permanently marking the texts. This strategy provides students with visual cues and tactile interaction with the texts, helping them to stay more actively engaged in the reading,

What to Do

1. Obtain four colors of Highlighter Tape (see Appendix D, *Where to Purchase Materials*).

2. Assign each story element or expository element a color, for example:
    Main idea = Pink
    Event = Yellow
    Character = Green
    Setting = Orange

3. Place strips of Highlighter Tape of each color on index cards (one index card for each student).

4. Provide each student with an index card of Highlighter Tape to use while reading.

5. Direct students to highlight story elements with the correct color tape as they read.

6. Hand out photocopies of Reproducible 5.2a, *Story Elements Graphic Organizer* for students to complete with colored pencils after reading and highlighting the text.

Consider

○ Sometimes students have more success if they begin with just one color of Highlighter Tape and one story element. As they become successful with the strategy, increase the expectations.

○ Highlighter Tape can be used to highlight almost any component of text—unknown words, misspelled words, vocabulary words, important dates in history, key elements of word problems in math. Consider the possibilities!

Notes

43

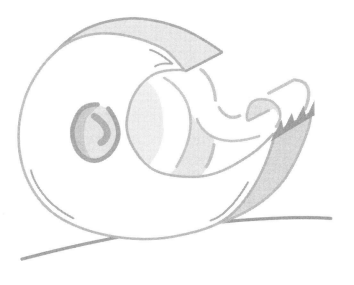

Strengthen Learning With Feedback Pipes

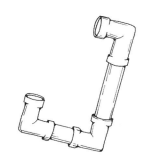

Standards Links

Reading: The student will hear, say, and manipulate phonemes.

Mathematics: The student will count by twos, fives, and tens to 100.

Foreign Language: The student will use the target language to engage in conversations.

Overview

In this strategy, a feedback loop amplifies the sound being made, thereby assisting students to focus and attend to important auditory information. Feedback pipes are made from PVC pipe to provide a feedback loop from a student's mouth to his or her ear. These tools also provide tactile learners with solid objects to hold while working with visual or auditory information.

Using his feedback pipe, Kengy amplifies the sound of his voice.

What to Do

1. Purchase PVC pipe from the plumbing supply section of your local hardware store. Using a hand saw, cut the pipe to the desired length and attach to elbow joints.

2. If individual students will have their own feedback pipes, use an indelible marker to write their names on the straight section of the pipes.

3. When it is time to intensify auditory feedback, direct students to use their feedback pipes, speaking softly into the mouthpiece while holding the receiving end to their ears.

Consider

⊃ Try using feedback pipes with students who like to read out loud, but who disturb classmates when they do so. These students will still get the auditory feedback they need, but will no longer bother others.

⊃ Feedback pipes can be very motivating for reluctant readers. Consider using them as a reward or motivational tool.

⊃ Math facts, or any other rote memorization, can be enhanced through auditory feedback.

⊃ Try "poetry pipes," "multiplication pipes," or "telephone number pipes."

Notes

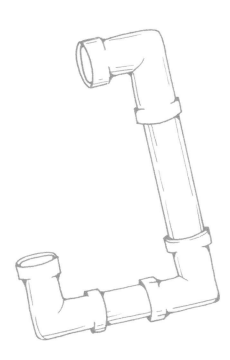

Making the Abstract Concrete With Colorful Cubes

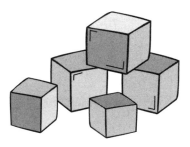

Standards Links

Writing: The student will write descriptive paragraphs, editing for proper grammar.

Lifelong Learning: The student will ask for and accept support.

Overview

Students create concrete representations of abstract elements using colorful cubes. Elements are color-coded to correspond to the colorful cubes, so students build hands-on models of the concepts you are teaching.

What to Do

1. Obtain a number of connecting cubes, such as Unifix Cubes, in various colors. (See Appendix D, *Where to Purchase Materials*.)

2. Develop a legend that links a color with a lesson element. If you are teaching students to write an organized paragraph, the legend might be:

   Main idea = Green

   Supporting details = Yellow

   Conclusion = Red

3. Provide a sample paragraph and ask students to build the paragraph with their colorful cubes, placing the correct color for each element in order from start to finish. For example, in the student writing sample in *Figure 5.1*, students begin building with one green cube, then they connect three yellow cubes and finish with a red one.

> *Figure 5.1*, Student writing sample
>
> I am going to do three things over vacation. I am going to watch lots of television. When I get bored with that, I'll play basketball with my friends. If they can't play, then I'll spend time with my dog. These three things should keep me busy during my time off.

4. Have students check their work by comparing their models to yours, or by working with partners.

Consider

 ➲ Provide each student with three cubes—green, yellow, and red. Students keep the cubes on the corners of their desks. If learning is going smoothly for them, they keep the green block on top. Yellow indicates "I have a question when you get a chance," and red indicates "I'm stuck until you help me."

 ➲ Colorful cubes can also help students follow a schedule. Color-code the subjects or periods of the day, for example:

History = Orange

Math = Blue

Reading = Red

Science = Green

Special periods = Brown

Writing = Yellow

➲ As students complete each period, they can connect another colored piece, until all the cubes are connected. (Time to go home!)

Notes

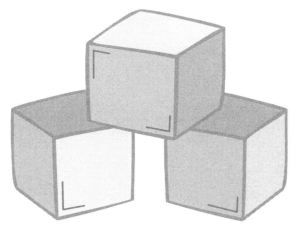

Better Retention With Note-Taking Quilts

Standards Links

Science: The student will understand biological evolution and the diversity of life.

Social Studies: The student will explain how massive immigration transformed American life.

Reading: The student will reflect on what has been learned from reading.

Overview

For students who do not have strong linguistic skills, this strategy is a wonderful alternative to traditional note-taking. Students summarize their learning with simple, symbolic drawings. As this patchwork of pictures comes together, students have a sequential structure to help them understand and retain key concepts.

What to Do

1. Determine how many times during a lesson or unit you will want students to summarize their learning.

2. Photocopy Reproducible 5.3, *Note-Taking Quilt*, and hand out to students.

3. At the designated intervals, direct students to stop and draw a simple summary of what they have learned in the "patch." Allow students one or two minutes to complete their drawings.

4. After each new "patch" is added, ask students to quickly and silently review the previous patches. This helps them connect their most recent learning with past learning.

Consider

- ○ Have students share their note-taking quilts with a partner or small group, explaining each "patch." Teaching others will boost their own retention.

- ○ Direct or help students to label each picture with a single word or phrase to capture its essence linguistically.

Notes

Organize Information With Graphic Organizers

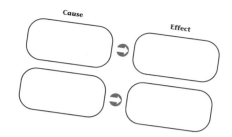

Standards Links

Writing: The student will write for a variety of purposes, organizing information to fit the purpose.

Social Studies: The student will describe how specific decisions and events had an impact on history.

Science: The student will understand and follow a process of scientific inquiry.

Overview

Graphic organizers are pictorial worksheets that help students organize information in nonlinear formats. They combine linguistic information with visual information, leading to greater long-term retention.

What to Do

1. Review your instructional content and choose the graphic organizer that most closely matches the structure of the information (see Reproducibles 5.2a–5.2e). For example, if you are teaching a social studies lesson about the causes of westward expansion, you might use Reproducible 5.2c, *Cause & Effect Graphic Organizer*. The graphic organizers included in the Reproducibles Section are:
    5.2a, *Story Elements*
    5.2b, *Process/Sequence*
    5.2c, *Cause & Effect*
    5.2d, *Main Idea/Supporting Details*
    5.2e, *Venn Diagram*

2. Make copies of the graphic organizer you select, and distribute to students.

3. Demonstrate on an overhead projector, chart pad, or blackboard how to complete the graphic organizer by filling in one or more sections.

4. Have students work independently or in pairs to complete the graphic organizer.

5. Encourage students to review their graphic organizers prior to quizzes and tests.

Consider

➲ Provide students with blank copies of each type of graphic organizer. Encourage students to use them when they are watching an educational video or listening to discussion in class, even if note-taking is not required. The act of jotting down ideas in a graphic format helps students retain information. It also keeps their attention during long periods of visual and auditory information.

➲ Adapt the graphic organizers to specific lessons by adding titles, computer clip art, or additional spaces.

➲ Once students become familiar with graphic organizers, ask them to design their own. Add their designs to your classroom collection for all students to use. Be sure to put the student designer's name on the master copy so that other students can ask for explanations if necessary.

Notes

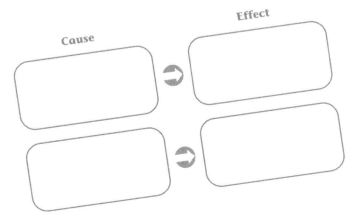

"I Spy" Quilts for Language Acquisition

Standards Links

Reading: The student will hear, say, and manipulate phonemes.

Writing: The student will expand and use vocabulary to describe people, places, and things.

Lifelong Learning: The student will gain and apply study skills (visual searching).

Foreign Language: The student will use basic vocabulary to describe items in the environment.

Overview

"I spy" quilts are based on the popular *I Spy* book series (Marzollo and Wick 1996). These simple patchwork quilts combine dozens of colorful pictures in a cozy, reassuring medium. By using an "I spy" quilt, you encourage language acquisition, matching of names with pictures, and many other emergent reading skills.

What to Do

1. Make, purchase, or convince a quilter to make an "I spy" quilt, following the directions provided in Reproducible 5.4a, *Quick and Simple Instructions for Making an "I Spy" Quilt*. Quilt kits are also available. (See Appendix D, *Where to Purchase Materials*.)

2. Offer students the "I spy" quilt to explore. Depending on the skills you want to focus on, ask students to:
   - Find/touch a picture of something that begins with "s".
   - Find/touch a picture of something that ends with "d".
   - Find/touch a picture of something you use in the kitchen.
   - Find/touch a picture of something that has two syllables.
   - Find/touch a picture next to, under, to the right of ….
   - Find/touch the picture of the _____.

3. You can turn this into an independent activity by writing your directions on a worksheet. Number each direction. Then ask students to write the direction number in the corresponding box of Reproducible 5.4b, *My Quilt*.

Consider

⊃ This activity can be especially effective with students who are fascinated by detailed pictures. Many teachers have had success using "I spy" quilts with students with autism.

⊃ "I spy" quilts are an effective tool for teaching students to scan or skim material using a structured approach. Ask students to find a specific object. Time them, and record how long it takes to find the object. Challenge students to scan more effectively (and more quickly!) by sweeping from left to right, and top to bottom. Have a student use a stopwatch to record times.

Notes

Independent Practice With Fact Flippers

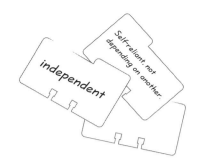

Standards Links

Mathematics: The student will compare and convert units of measure for length, weight, and volume within the U.S. Customary system and with the metric system.

Reading: The student will read and learn the meanings of unfamiliar words.

Technology: The student will know characteristics and uses of a computer's special function keys.

Overview

This strategy can be applied to any materials a student is required to memorize. It provides intense tactile input as students flip through facts in a novel way. It also gives students practice in responding to questions in random order, thus strengthening retention.

What to Do

1. Obtain a circular Rolodex to turn into a fact flipper.

2. On each Rolodex card, place your prompt and answer. For example, place a math problem on one side and the answer on the opposite side, upside down. Or, try a vocabulary word on one side, and the definition on the opposite side, upside down. To help students learn the function keys of a computer, write the key on one side of the card and its function on the other.

3. Choose a student to spin the fact flipper.

4. When the fact flipper stops, the student asks himself or herself the question on top and tries to answer it correctly.

5. The student self-checks by flipping the card over to read the answer on the back.

Consider

➲ Before buying a circular Rolodex, ask friends, families, and coworkers if they have an old one that they might donate to the classroom.

➲ Suggest that parents make fact flippers at home to support their children's study and homework activities.

Notes

Interactive Learning With Match 'Em Up Books

Standards Links

Reading: The student will apply knowledge of how print is organized and read.

Reading: The student will apply word analysis skills to ensure proper grammar usage.

 Lifelong Learning: The student will demonstrate time management skills.

Overview

Simple ways to make textbooks more interactive are a boon when working with struggling learners. In this strategy, students move words from place to place on the pages of a book, matching or labeling selected words.

What to Do

1. Choose several simple texts that are bound with a staple in the middle of the pages. Texts with one line of print per page work best.

2. Remove the staples and laminate the pages with a heavy duty laminate.

3. Three-hole punch these pages and place them in a three-ring binder.

4. Adhere the loop side of a self-sticking Velcro fastener under each word in the text.

5. Type the words from the book into a word processing program, using the same font and making them approximately the same size. Laminate these pages.

6. Cut out each individual word from the laminated word pages. Adhere the hook side of a Velcro fastener to the back side of each word. Be sure that the fastener is the mate to the pieces you placed in the book (i.e., hook vs. loop).

7. Have students match the individual words to the corresponding words in the text and attach them.

Consider

⊃ Instead of having students match words, you can adapt this activity for parts of speech. Type and laminate several copies of the various parts of speech (noun, verb, adjective, etc.). Cut out each individual word. Adhere a fastener to the back. Ask students to label each word in the text with a part of speech.

⊃ You can create Match 'Em Up schedules as well as books. They can be a highly effective way of helping tactile learners get organized. To create a schedule:

1. Type a list of the activities the student typically participates in throughout the day (for nonreaders, use pictures or symbols that represent these activities, or copy Reproducible 5.5a through 5.5d, *Match 'Em Up Daily Activities*).

2. Laminate the words or pictures and cut them out.

3. Apply a small Velcro fastener to the back of each.

4. Photocopy Reproducible 5.5b, *Match 'Em Up Daily Schedule.*

5. Laminate the blank schedule and attach fasteners down the right hand column.

6. Together, you can organize a daily schedule by affixing and removing activities throughout the day.

Notes

Boost Fluency With Colored Strips

Standards Links

Reading: The student will read aloud familiar stories, poems, and passages with fluency and expression (rhythm, flow, meter, tempo).

 Lifelong Learning: The student will maintain attention to text material.

Overview

Students use colored strips of acetate to temporarily highlight text material as they are reading, improving focus and fluency. The strips also provide tactile input as students move them down the page.

What to Do

1. Obtain several project folders or report covers made of transparent colored acetate. (See Appendix D, *Where to Purchase Materials*.)

2. Cut the acetate into strips that are wide enough to cover two lines of text in the chosen book. Be sure the strips include the fold from the edge of the report cover so that it can wrap around the page.

3. Ask students to choose colored strips. (Encourage students to try various colors during the first few days to determine which colors work best for them.)

4. Direct students to place the colored strips over their book pages, one half on the back of the page, one half on the front.

5. Have each student line up the colored strip with the sentence about to be read. The strip should highlight two lines of text at once.

6. As students read, direct them to move their strips down the page, continually covering the line they are reading. This will help them to keep their place, reading more fluently as they move from line to line.

Consider

⟳ If students have individual, printed schedules, they can use colored strips to track their progress throughout the day.

Notes

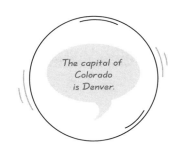

The capital of Colorado is Denver.

Mastering Content With the Info Ball Game

Standards Links

Social Studies: The student will know the location of places and geographic features.

Lifelong Learning: The student will use effective oral communication skills in group activities.

Mathematics: The student will use basic and advanced procedures while performing the processes of computation.

Overview

This multimodality, high-energy strategy engages students in practicing curriculum content. Students use their imaginations to "throw" content to each other. While practicing content in this way, students are also improving their visual and auditory attending skills.

What to Do

1. Ask students to stand in a circle.

2. Begin the game by announcing the topic (e.g., state facts, math facts, or science vocabulary and definitions).

3. Have one student start by making eye contact with a student across the circle.

4. Once eye contact is made, the student "throws" the information "ball" to the student across from him or her. For example, if the topic is Colorado state facts, the student might throw "The capital of Colorado is Denver." Have students use their throwing arms to simulate the throwing of a ball as they "throw" information to each other.

5. The receiver "catches" the information by simulating a physical catch, and repeating the information (e.g., "The capital of Colorado is Denver").

6. Now that student takes a turn. He or she makes eye contact with someone else in the circle and throws that person a new fact.

7. The game proceeds at rapid fire pace.

8. If a student throws incorrect information, pause the game. Tell the student the correct information, or ask for another student to help out.

Consider

➲ Many topics lend themselves to this game, including foreign language equivalents, story elements, parts of speech, vocabulary words and definitions, and science facts.

➲ To make the game more challenging, you can play it so that the thrower does not include the answer. For example, one student "throws" 2 + 2. Then the catcher has to answer correctly "4." If you play the game this way, be sensitive to the differing ability levels in the group, so that struggling students are not publicly embarrassed.

Notes

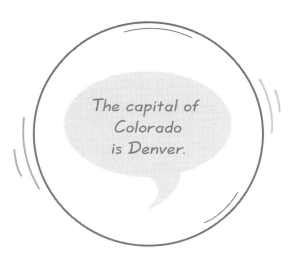

Expand Thinking With "Roll the Cube"

Standards Links

Writing: The student will write descriptive paragraphs that elaborate on the central idea.

Reading: The student will analyze and evaluate information from a variety of sources.

Overview

This hands-on approach encourages students to extend their thinking and learning. Cubes provide a level of unpredictability that promotes flexibility and creativity. Students often demonstrate increased motivation for learning when they use the cubes.

What to Do

1. Collect two 8-ounce milk cartons from the school cafeteria and wash them thoroughly.

2. Cut off the tops of the milk cartons at the line where the upward sloping angle begins.

3. Insert one carton into the other, gently pushing them together until they form a cube.

4. Cover the cube with plain adhesive paper or other plain paper.

5. Cut six paper squares, 3" x 3" each. On each square, write a prompt. For example, for writing extenders, you might choose from those listed in *Figure 5.2*.

Figure 5.2: Prompts for writing extension cubes.

Writing Extenders

- Suddenly ...
- Just then ...
- By coincidence ...
- If only ...
- Perhaps ...
- Could it be ...
- Afterward ...
- Just in time ...
- Saved by ...
- In order to ...
- In other words ...
- Once again ...
- Through the eyes of ...
- The next day ...
- Surprisingly ...
- In the beginning ...

6. Adhere the six prompts to the sides of the cube.

7. Ask students to take turns rolling the cube. Students integrate the prompt from the top of the cube into their writing.

Consider

⊃ You can make cubes of various levels of difficulty to match the diversity of abilities in your classroom. You might make blue cubes that include basic skill prompts. Green cubes could include prompts for students working at an advanced level.

⊃ Question cubes have broad application in classrooms. On each face of the cube, write one of the six question words (who, what, when, where, why, how). You or your students can roll the question cube and generate questions about the content you are currently teaching. For example, during a discussion of a novel, let's say a student rolls a "why." She then generates the question, "Why do you think the author chose to use that voice in his writing?"

⊃ Use your own ideas for cubes. Students might roll cubes to determine which reading strategy to try, to decide which study skill method to use for homework, or to settle on a conflict resolution technique. Be creative!

Notes

Teach Categorization Skills With the Silent Sort Game

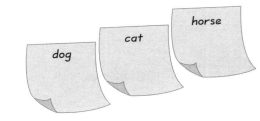

Standards Links

Science: The student will investigate and understand that organisms are made of cells and have distinguishing characteristics.

Science: The student will investigate and understand that objects can be described in terms of their physical properties.

Writing: The student will organize ideas in a logical manner.

Overview

The ability to identify similarities and differences is an essential skill. The Silent Sort strategy encourages students to thoughtfully categorize information, quietly grouping information on the wall or blackboard. Students utilize their visual, tactile, and kinesthetic modalities.

What to Do

1. Give each student a sticky note.

2. Ask students to write on their sticky notes one example of the information you are teaching. For example, if you are teaching about animals, each student would write one animal each on their sticky notes.

3. Explain the entire game to the class, demonstrating as you explain. Tell them that the game is to be done in complete silence. When you say "go," students go to the blackboard (or wall space) and stick up their animal notes. As they see other students' notes go up, they are to begin to group the notes according to similarities. For example, with animals, one student might stick up "cat." Another student might stick up "horse," nearby. Yet another student might stick up "bee," but in another location, beginning a new group. After placing their own notes on the board, students are to look at the other notes. If they see a note that might be better grouped elsewhere, they move it. Once a student feels that all the notes are grouped correctly, he or she sits down.

4. In this version of the game, you do not provide predetermined categories for students; therefore Silent Sort may lead to common groupings or unexpected groupings. If you desire specific categories, write them on the blackboard prior to the sorting.

5. When all the students are satisfied with the sort and seated, lead a discussion. Questions might include:
- What names might you give these groups?
- What do all the animals in this group have in common?
- Why did you include this animal in this group?
- What other animals could you include in this group that are not already there?
- Are there other ways these animals could be grouped?
- What did you like/dislike about this game?

Consider

⮑ You can play Silent Sort at the beginning of the school year as a way to get to know each other. Direct each student to write his or her name and a favorite hobby or interest on a sticky note. Have students sort the notes according to common interests.

⮑ Arrange information for reports, newspapers, or other lengthy writing projects by playing Silent Sort. This is especially effective in group projects when individual students have differing ideas about how the information should be arranged.

⮑ Individuals can use Silent Sort on their desktops. Instead of writing just one example on one note, direct students to write 10 – 20 notes. Using these, they can sort into their own categories or into categories you determine.

Notes

Improve Comprehension With Sticky Summaries

Standards Links

Reading: The student will paraphrase information found in nonfiction materials.

 Lifelong Learning: The student will gain and apply study skills and learning strategies for managing self.

Overview

This strategy teaches students how to succinctly summarize what they have read. It also provides a study aide for reviewing and memorizing textbook information.

What to Do

1. Provide each student with one package of small sticky notes.

2. Ask students to read a page in their textbooks.

3. Direct them to summarize the page in one word or in a short phrase. Have them write the summary on a sticky note.

4. Show students how to place their sticky notes on the top, right hand edges of their pages, forming a tab.

5. For each successive page, students follow Steps 2 – 4, placing each successive tab lower than its predecessor.

6. When studying, students review their Sticky Summaries for important ideas from the text. When looking for specific information, they can also quickly find the correct page (especially helpful during open book tests!).

Consider

- ➲ Place sticky summaries at the end of each paragraph or section of information, rather than at the end of the page.

- ➲ Suggest to students that they use Sticky Summaries on each page of notes they take in class. This will aid their efforts to study for tests.

Notes

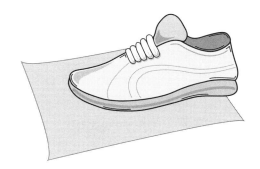

Wake 'Em Up With Stepping Stones

Standards Links

Social Studies: The student will describe the ideas and events of the 1920s, 1930s, and 1940s in the United States.

Mathematics: The student will round whole numbers to the nearest tens and hundreds.

Mathematics: The student will identify relevant properties of plane and solid geometric figures.

Overview

Novelty is a proven way to grab attention. This strategy uses novelty to gain students' attention and provides a simple method for review of key information.

What to Do

1. Determine the information you wish students to review and retain. Choose three to five facts. For example, in history, choose three to five critical dates students need to remember.

2. Print each date on a separate 8½" x 11" sheet of paper. Laminate each sheet for durability or insert into clear plastic page covers. These are your stepping stones.

3. After students have entered the class and are engaged in a student-directed activity, step outside the door into the hallway. Tape the stepping stones onto the floor in the direction that students will exit the classroom.

4. As students line up to leave at the end of class, tell them that they must step on each stepping stone as they exit and give the correct answer. In the history example, students stand on the date and state the event associated with it.

Consider

⊃ Use stepping stones in the morning when students arrive for class. It's a great way to stimulate the brain!

⊃ Use stepping stones for a special thought for the day. Place each word of the thought or quote on a sheet of paper. If students will be stepping around them, rather than on them, they do not need to be laminated.

⊃ Have students generate ideas for stepping stones. As students develop their ideas, they will think about important concepts and determine which are most critical to review (which is a review in itself!).

Notes

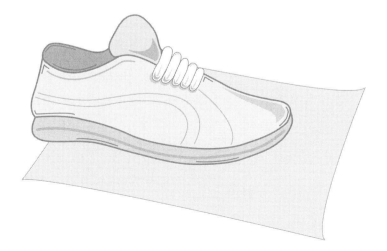

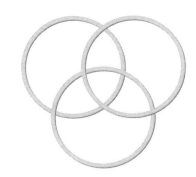

Compare and Contrast With Hula Hoops

Standards Links

Social Studies: The student will compare his or her own state to states from various regions of the country.

Science: The student will compare and contrast results of various investigations.

 Lifelong Learning: The student will demonstrate socially acceptable behavior.

Overview

A Venn diagram is a graphic organizer that shows similarities and differences between two or three things. When you use Hula Hoops to form Venn diagrams, you increase student attention, motivation, and success.

What to Do

1. Obtain three or more Hula Hoops. (Check with your physical education department. They may have several you can borrow.)

2. If you are using three Hula Hoops, place them flat on the floor in a Venn diagram formation (see Reproducible 5.2e, *Venn Diagram*).

3. Using three index cards, write the names of the three things being compared. For example, if you are comparing states, you might write "California," "New York," and "Florida."

4. Place one index card in each hoop.

5. Ask students to identify a characteristic of one of the states. As they volunteer, direct each student to stand in the Hula Hoop for the correct state and say the characteristic. For example, a student might stand in the California hoop and say "west coast" or stand in the overlap between Florida and New York and say "east coast."

6. If you have many hoops, you can divide the class into smaller groups, giving each group three hoops.

7. Following the kinesthetic part of this activity, have students summarize their learning on Reproducible 5.2e, *Venn Diagram*, or on a Venn diagram that you've created on your own.

Consider

➲ Individual students can make Venn diagrams out of pipe cleaners, key rings, or Wikki Stix.

➲ Grab students' attention at the beginning of class by trying to Hula Hoop! Or, use it as a motivator. Tell students that you will Hula Hoop at the end of class if they pay attention, develop good products, etc.

➲ Use the hoops to talk about personal space and social distance issues. Students can learn that in American culture, if you are closer to a person than the distance of a hoop, then you are in their personal space. Discuss when this is appropriate and when it is not.

➲ Use individual hoops as "containers" for sorting and categorizing information. For example, write words from a paragraph you are reading on index cards. Label the hoops "verbs," "nouns," etc. Direct students to place the word cards in the correct hoop.

Notes

71

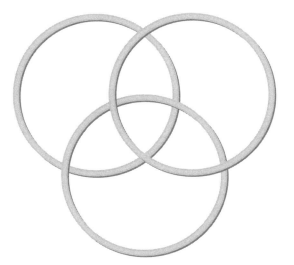

Teach Spelling and Vocabulary With "Sign and Spell"

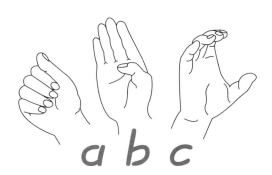

Standards Links

Writing: The student will correctly spell frequently used words.

Writing: The student will write for a variety of purposes, selecting vocabulary to enhance the central idea and voice.

Overview

Learning and retaining the correct spelling of new words is a challenge for many students. By involving a tactile response, in the form of sign language, multiple memory paths are activated. This increases the likelihood of retention.

What to Do

1. Obtain a sign language resource such as *The Joy of Signing* (Riekehof 1987).

2. Over the course of several weeks, teach students how to sign the alphabet. (See the sidebar that follows.)

3. When students have mastered the alphabet, begin to integrate it in your spelling program. During the first week, assign students to finger spell a few of their spelling words for homework. As students become increasingly comfortable with signing, increase the expectation until they are finger spelling all of their words.

4. Over the next few weeks, integrate finger spelling into content areas as you introduce new vocabulary. For example, during a class discussion of body systems, you might ask students to finger spell "cardiovascular."

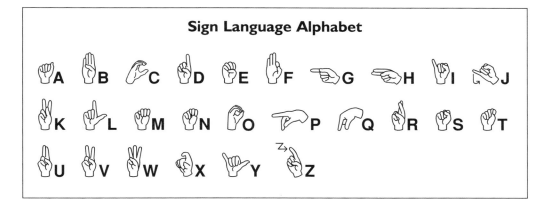

Sign Language Alphabet

Consider

↻ In addition to finger spelling, use Reproducible 5.6, *Sign and Spell* to teach signs for each spelling word. Add the signs from your sign language resource in the right hand column, and direct students to practice the sign as they practice the word.

Notes

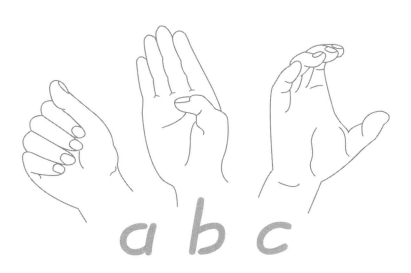

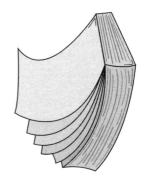

Make Math More Meaningful With Fact Family Triangles

Standards Links

Mathematics: The student will demonstrate conceptual meanings for the operations of multiplication and division.

Mathematics: The student will demonstrate proficiency with basic multiplication and division facts without the use of a calculator.

Overview

Math facts become more meaningful when students understand the concept of "fact families" and that numbers are flexible. This strategy teaches both of these ideas, while providing tactile input as students practice math facts.

What to Do

1. Obtain several packages of 3" x 3" sticky notes.

2. Pull a sticky note from the stack and fold it in half diagonally to make a triangle.

3. In the center of the triangle write +/- (for addition and subtraction facts) or x/÷ (for multiplication and division facts).

Fact Families

Fact families are sets of three numbers that can be interchanged to form mathematical equations. For example 3, 4, and 12 can form the following equations:

$$3 \times 4 = 12$$
$$4 \times 3 = 12$$
$$12 \div 3 = 4$$
$$12 \div 4 = 3$$

4. On the three corners of the triangle, write the three numbers in the fact family as in *Figure 5.3*. For example, 3, 4, and 12 are a multiplication/division fact family. (To conserve sticky notes, write a fact family on both sides of the sticky note.)

Figure 5.3: Fact family triangles

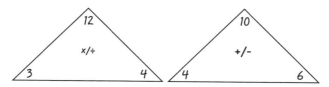

5. After making a set of fact family triangles, direct students to pick one. Ask students to place their right or left thumbs and forefingers on one corner, covering that number and leaving two numbers uncovered. Students manipulate the visible numbers to form and solve a math fact. For example, if a student covers 4, leaving 12 and 3, he or she would say "12 ÷ 3 = 4."

6. When students solve the first problem, they rotate the triangle and form another fact from the same family (e.g., "3 x 4 = 12").

7. Continue through the entire set of fact family triangles you created.

Consider

⟳ Have students make their own sets of fact family triangles. This serves as a review before they even begin to play with their triangles.

⟳ Color-coding may help some students be more successful. Try writing the largest number in a different color than the two smaller numbers.

Notes

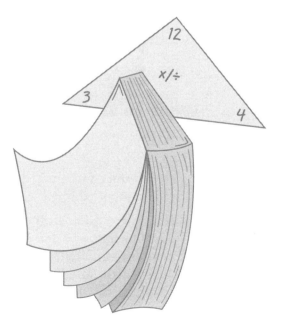

Increase Fluency and Comprehension by "Chunking"

Standards Links

Reading: The student will independently read and follow detailed directions in paragraph form.

Reading: The student will independently read with appropriate fluency to enhance comprehension.

Lifelong Learning: The student will attend to important details in printed text.

Overview

"Chunking" is a strategy that the human brain naturally uses to divide large pieces of information into pieces small enough to comprehend and retain. While chunking is an important strategy for memorization, it can also be applied to increase reading fluency. In this strategy, students focus on small bits of content within a larger context, so that they can achieve fluency and comprehension in their reading.

Kengy uses his chunking frame for better fluency.

What to Do

1. Obtain a piece of cardboard or heavy weight paper (file folders work, too).

2. Cut the cardboard into the shape of a short, fat capital T (approximately 3" x 3").

3. Cut a window in the middle of the T, as shown in the illustration. The window, when placed over text, should be wide enough to expose approximately five words, and high enough to expose just one line of text. The size of your window depends on the size of the type in your grade-level texts.

4. Direct students to place the "chunking frame" over the words as they read. The chunking frames expose several words. Encourage students to "chunk" those words, or group them together, reading them as smoothly as they can as a single group.

5. Have students read the same chunk of words as many times as they need to in order to read them smoothly as a group.

6. When students are finished reading an entire sentence, tell them to remove the chunking frame and read the entire sentence as fluently as possible.

Consider

⟳ Make chunking frames of various sizes. Allow students to use them to focus in on specific math problems or vocabulary words on worksheets.

⟳ Encourage students to use chunking frames when studying for tests. For example, rather than looking at an entire list of spelling words or algorithms, students can chunk together a few at a time.

Notes

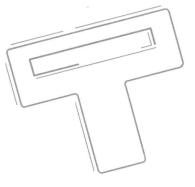

Develop Automaticity With Musical Spelling

Standards Links

Writing: The student will write to communicate ideas, using correct spelling for frequently used words.

Writing: The student will accurately use spelling words (district grade level list) in writing.

Overview

Brain researchers tell us that language and music are closely linked in the brain, even sharing some of the same neural circuits. By combining music with semantic learning, we can increase our ability to retain information and increase automaticity. This strategy does just that! It provides a way for students to associate very specific musical input with the accurate spelling of words.

Zak plays his spelling words.

What to Do

1. Obtain a small, musical keyboard from your music department or a local toy store. (They are usually under $10.)

2. Obtain small sticker dots or labels that will fit on the size of the keys.

3. On each dot, write a letter of the alphabet. You may wish to write vowels on dots of a different color.

4. Stick the dots on the keys in alphabetical order, placing the vowels on black keys, and the consonants on white keys.

5. Call on a student to spell a word and say it aloud as he or she presses the corresponding key on the keyboard. Have the student repeat this at least two more times. If working with a group, ask several students to play the same word before moving on to the next spelling word. Each word will have its own unique tune. Students can sing along!

Consider

⟳ For individual work it is helpful to have a piano keyboard that has a plug for earphones!

⟳ Suggest this strategy to parents for home spelling practice.

Notes

Improve Performance With Self-Monitoring Systems

Standards Links

Writing: The student will add or substitute sentences to clarify and enhance meaning.

Reading: The student will use a variety of reading strategies to read and understand text.

Lifelong Learning: The student will use self-regulation techniques to enhance learning opportunities.

Physical Education: The student will participate in activities that develop physical endurance.

Overview

Before we can improve a behavior or skill, we have to be aware of it. Many students do not demonstrate strong self-awareness; that is, they often don't have an accurate sense of what or how well they are doing. Self-monitoring systems increase awareness of skills and behaviors and help students see their progress.

What to Do

1. Choose areas that you feel students need help in, but that students are not aware of needing help in. For example, many students are not aware of the length of their writing pieces. You may choose to set up a self-monitoring system that asks students to track the number of sentences they write.

2. Develop a simple tracking system. Reproducible 5.7, *Self-Monitoring Chart* provides a bar graph that sends a strong visual message to students. Simply recording tally marks or numbers works just as well though. Students keep their records in their notebooks or on a corner of their desks.

3. Explain that students will be monitoring themselves. For the chosen task, students track the levels of accomplishment. For example, when finished writing, students count the number of sentences (or the average number of words per sentence) and record the number for the day on their charts.

4. Continue self-monitoring for at least two weeks, reminding students as necessary.

5. At the end of the first week, sit with students and review their charts. Ask them to tell you what they see. Did they improve? What days were better? Why? By having students analyze the results themselves you increase their self-awareness.

Consider

 ➲ Because of the nature of self-monitoring, it is best *not* to link it with consequence systems. A positive or negative consequence in the offing may entice students to be dishonest as they monitor themselves.

➲ Self-monitoring systems are effective in increasing on-task behavior. Many struggling students have high levels of off-task behavior and are unaware of it. Before improving their behavior, they must be aware of it! If you use self-monitoring for on-task behavior, simply cue students at random intervals throughout the day to "check" themselves.

Notes

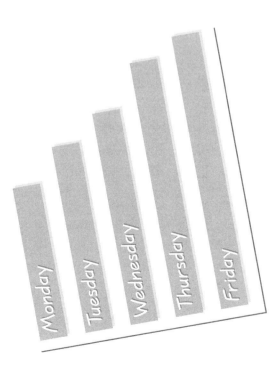

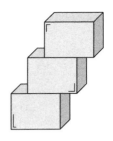

Make Complex Concepts Easier to Understand With Symbol Blocks

Standards Links

Science: The student will investigate and understand that living things are part of a system and are interdependent with their living and nonliving surroundings.

Social Studies: The student will explain the fundamental ideals and principles that form the foundation of our government.

Overview

Many students find abstract concepts difficult to comprehend. For these students, it is helpful to make the material as concrete as possible. This strategy encourages students to build concrete representations of their learning, thereby making it more meaningful.

Mavi builds her representation of "interdependence."

What to Do

1. Obtain a bucket of Lego or similar building blocks. For students in third through sixth grades, the smallest blocks are usually best. (Ask families if they have any interlocking blocks at home that could be donated.)

2. After you teach a complex concept in class, such as interdependence, ask students to form small groups.

3. Give each group a large handful of blocks (assorted sizes, colors, and shapes).

4. Direct the groups to build symbolic representations of what they learned in the lesson. Allow 3 – 5 minutes for students to complete their task. See *Figure 5.4*.

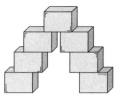

"Interdependence"

living things depend upon their nonliving environment.

5. When all groups are finished, ask each to explain the group's representation and how it relates to the concepts taught in the lesson.

Consider

◒ Give symbol blocks to individual students, rather than to groups. Each student can build his or her own interpretation of the concept. These can then be shared in small groups.

◒ Save what your students build and put them on display in the classroom (great for school open houses!).

◒ Suggest that parents and students try this strategy at home. Students may build symbols that show what was taught in class or may build representations of the homework reading.

Notes

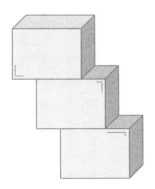

Teach Structures Kinesthetically With the Powder Walk

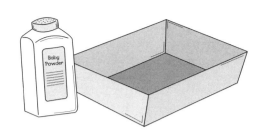

Standards Links

Social Studies: The student will describe the U.S. as composed of states and locate and name states in his or her own geographic region.

Health: The student will know the basic structure of the human body.

Overview

The saying "walk a mile in my shoes" is fitting. Many learners understand something better after they have walked it. In this strategy students walk through the material being studied, leaving paths as they go.

What to Do

1. Place two cups of baby powder or flour in a large, shallow, flat box (approximately $1\frac{1}{2}'$ x $2\frac{1}{2}'$).

2. Take students outside to a paved area. Using chalk, draw an outline of the material being studied. For example, in geography class you might draw an outline of the United States; in science you might draw the human heart.

3. Ask a student to step into the box of baby powder, so that the bottoms of both feet are coated.

4. Direct the student to walk the path being studied. For example, the student might walk the path of the Oregon Trail. In science, the student might walk through the chambers of the heart in the direction of the blood flow.

5. As the student walks, a powder trail will be left behind. Depending on the content, you may choose to have each student "powder walk" behind the first, forming a train.

Consider

➲ Younger students can "powder walk" letters, numbers, shapes, etc.

Notes

85

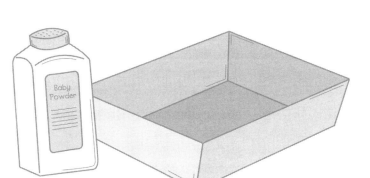

Help Students Find Answers With Grabbers

Standards Links

Writing: The student will be able to identify the parts of speech, such as nouns, pronouns, verbs, adverbs, adjectives, conjunctions, prepositions, and interjections.

Mathematics: The student will recognize, draw, describe, and analyze geometric shapes in one, two, and three dimensions.

Overview

Brain research shows that our attention is drawn to movement. Adding movement to the material you present on an overhead projector results in increased attention. In addition, this strategy provides kinesthetic learners with opportunities to get up and interact with the information displayed on the overhead.

What to Do

1. Gather sheets of cardboard or posterboard in neon colors.

2. Cut the cardboard into various shapes. Standard shapes include a circle (approximately 12" in diameter), a large rectangle (approximately 4" x 18"), and a small rectangle (approximately 4" x 6"). Other simple shapes might be cut to align with the content you are teaching. For example, you might cut out a star if you are teaching astronomy, an apple if you are teaching health, or a heart if you are teaching poetry. These shapes, your "grabbers," can be kept with your overhead projector cart.

3. Develop transparencies that support your instruction. These might include copies of a page from the text, a note-taking outline, vocabulary and definitions, geometric shapes, or questions and answers.

4. Determine your focus. Do you want students to find the correct answer? Find an adverb? Find an important date? Find the main sentence of the paragraph?

5. Call on a student to take a grabber and approach the screen. Ask the student to "grab" the answer to your question by placing the grabber against the screen in the correct location. The answer will then be projected onto the grabber. The neon-colored grabber will make the information look highlighted.

6. Once the information is "grabbed," tell the student to bring it to you. As the student walks toward you, holding out the grabber, the information will become larger, making it look to students as if it is moving toward them.

Consider

- ⊃ Each student can make and keep a grabber at his or her own desk.
- ⊃ Depending on the height of your students, you may need to project the material they need to "grab" so that it is near the bottom of the screen.

Notes

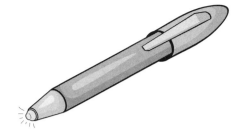

Improve Writing Skills With Light Pens

Standards Links

Writing: The student will be able to write stories, letters, and reports with greater detail and supporting material.

Writing: The student will be able to create documents with legible handwriting.

Writing: The student will edit and revise written work.

Overview

You can increase student motivation and focus while writing using light pens. This strategy increases the visual and tactile input a student receives, resulting in longer, more focused written work.

What to Do

1. Obtain a Nite Companion pen light from the hardware, automotive, or office supply area of your local department store (or see Appendix D, *Where to Purchase Materials*).

2. Meet with individual students quietly. Work with each student to set goals, such as to increase the length of their written work or maintain a clearer focus. Explain that the pen light will help.

3. As each student writes with the pen light, the flashlight in the tip will light up the immediate area around the letters being written.

4. To increase the power of the lighting, students can work in a darker area or you can turn off the overhead lights.

5. Track each student's progress toward the goal you set using Reproducible 5.7, *Self-Monitoring Chart*.

Consider

- ⟳ Obtain several light pens if possible. Allow the whole class to work in the dark during some of their writing assignments.

- ⟳ For editing, replace the pen cartridge with a different color ink.

- ⟳ Suggest that parents and students obtain pen lights to use at home. This can lead to improved written homework assignments.

- ⟳ If noticeable improvement occurs, use the pen during test-taking times. Check with your district and state authorities to determine if this would be an acceptable modification.

Notes

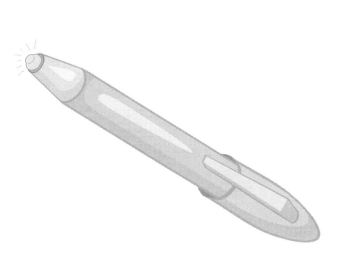

Reading, Measuring, and Analyzing With Wikki Stix

Standards Links

Reading: The student will discriminate between fact and opinion when reading text.

Mathematics: The student will make and use direct and indirect measurements to describe and compare objects in his or her environment.

Social Studies: The student will analyze historical text and identify key dates and events in state history.

Overview

Wikki Stix are strings covered in colored wax. They are bendable and shape-able, like pipe cleaners, but without the potentially dangerous wire in the center. Because Wikki Stix are coated in wax, they can stick to text book or worksheet pages. With them, students can creatively underline, circle, or highlight key information.

What to Do

1. Obtain Wikki Stix from toy stores or teacher resource stores. (See Appendix D, *Where to Purchase Materials*.)

2. When introducing Wikki Stix to your class, allow time for students to experiment with them. After this period, give each student one or two Wikki Stix.

3. When students are working with texts or worksheets, direct them to make a circle (or arrow or line) with their Wikki, highlighting the important information. Depending on the standard you are working toward, this might include:
   - Answer to a question
   - Directions
   - Important names or characters
   - Key dates
   - Known or unknown vocabulary words
   - Main idea of a paragraph
   - Parts of speech
   - Story elements
   - Supporting details
   - Vowel and consonant sounds

4. As students place the Wikki Stix on their papers and apply a bit of pressure, they will stick. Have students hold up their books so you can quickly scan the room for a quick, informal assessment.

5. Students can remove the Wikki Stix by gently pulling them off the pages.

6. Wikki Stix can also be used to measure objects (length, perimeter, angle). Students can stick one alongside the object, and then lay it along a ruler.

Consider

⟳ Store Wikki Stix in small plastic baggies. Be sure to collect the same number that you distributed, so that they do not inadvertently get left in textbooks.

 ⟳ A single Wikki is a wonderful device to keep fidgety hands occupied. You may find that tactile learners attend better to auditory instruction when they have Wikki Stix to manipulate.

Notes

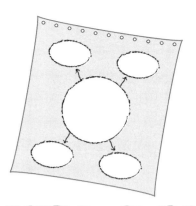

Step Up to Mastery With Hop-Step Mats

Standards Links

Mathematics: The student will demonstrate understanding and proficiency with basic addition and subtraction.

Writing: The student will organize written work using strategies such as lists, outlining, and appropriate graphic representations.

Writing: The student will spell frequently used words correctly, using phonics rules and exceptions.

Overview

In this strategy, you lay content information on the floor, and students physically move through it. The content information is written on a plastic shower curtain liner with permanent marker. Once this "hop-step" mat is on the floor, students can walk on it to review content.

What to Do

1. Obtain an inexpensive, plastic shower-curtain liner.

2. Using permanent markers, write or draw the content you want to teach on the shower curtain. For example, to practice basic addition and subtraction, make a grid of twenty boxes. In each, write a number from 1 – 20. For writing, draw a graphic organizer (see Reproducibles 5.2a–e). Be sure the shapes you draw are large enough to accommodate your students' feet.

3. Find a large open space on the floor and lay the mat down. Direct students to stand around the outside edges of it.

4. Call on one student at a time. Direct the students to step on the mat and walk or hop through the content while saying it aloud. For example, call out an addition problem (2 + 7) and direct the student to hop it out, also saying the equation aloud ("2 + 7 = 9"). For a writing activity with the graphic organizer used in Reproducible 5.2d, have the student stand in the middle to talk about the main idea, then hop or step to the peripheral areas to discuss supporting ideas.

5. When finished with the mat, fold it up and store it in a location where children cannot access it unsupervised.

Consider

- ➲ Cut shower curtains in half for smaller amounts of content (and to reduce the expense!).

- ➲ Make a hop-step mat of a computer keyboard. Students can practice spelling while reinforcing technology standards.

- ➲ Hop-step mats stay in place best on carpet. For added staying power, adhere small pieces of hook Velcro to the underside of each corner of the mat. If using a hop-step mat on hard surfaces, adhere small pieces of two-sided tape or non-skid shelf liner to each corner.

Notes

Meeting Standards

Neatness Counts!
Try Graph Paper

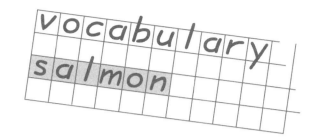

Standards Links

Mathematics: The student will link concepts and procedures as he or she develops and uses computational techniques.

Writing: The student will create readable documents with legible handwriting.

Overview

Many students who struggle in school appear disorganized, sloppy, and inattentive. These outward signs can be a clue to visual perception difficulties or attention deficits (or simple sloppiness!). Using graph paper, you can help these students to be successful.

What to Do

1. Obtain graph paper of various sizes. Make it accessible for students in the classroom.

2. Encourage students to use the graph paper when they are solving math problems that involve double digits or greater. Demonstrate on an overhead projector that each digit fits in a box on the graph, keeping digits lined up neatly and accurately.

3. You can also encourage students to use graph paper when writing. They can practice letter spacing by staying within the boxes on the graph paper.

Consider

➲ Use a highlighter to color in graph paper boxes that should contain numbers or letters. For example, color in six boxes horizontally if the vocabulary word is "salmon."

➲ Use graph paper when working with geometric shapes, maps, time lines, and measurements. Keep a supply handy at all times—you may find that your students develop new ways to use it.

Notes

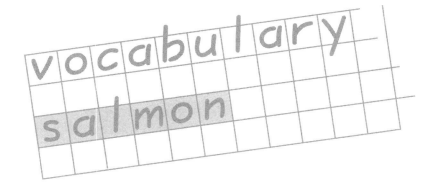

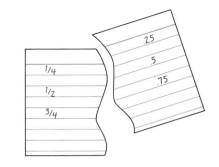

Generalize Learning With Go-Together Puzzles

Standards Links

Mathematics: The student will identify, describe, analyze, extend, and create a wide variety of patterns in numbers, shapes, and data.

Reading: The student will critically analyze and comprehend text by making connections to personal experience, other texts, and media.

Mathematics: The student will use the relationships among numbers in problem-solving situations by comparing fractions, decimals, and percents.

Overview

You can help students make connections between related ideas—an important skill for students generalizing learning in a wide variety of situations. This strategy utilizes simple two-piece puzzles, made by you or your students, to create physical connections between ideas.

What to Do

1. Obtain several dozen index cards and distribute three to five cards to each student.

2. Explain to students that while you discuss the content, they should think about the connections between ideas, or the "go-togethers." For example, in literature, students might look for text-to-text connections, such as between *Harry Potter and the Sorcerer's Stone* and *The Wizard of Oz*. In math, they might look for numeric equivalents or patterns, such as $1/4$ and .25.

3. As students think of connections, they write the first ideas on the left side of their index cards, and their second ideas on the right side.

4. When the discussion or lecture is complete, make sure that every student has developed at least three "go-togethers."

5. Direct students to cut their cards in half. They may cut a straight line (most difficult) or may use a jagged or curvy line (for easier matching).

6. Have students form small groups. Within each group, one student collects and shuffles the puzzle pieces.

7. Each group lays all the puzzle pieces on the floor (or on a table top) and see if they can make the connections.

8. When all the matches have been made, ask students if they noticed any cards that could be "go-togethers" with other cards.

9. Discuss the importance of connections in life outside the classroom.

Consider

⊃ Use go-together puzzles for vocabulary words and definitions.

⊃ These puzzles can be designed to talk about emotions. For example, a picture of a broken lamp on one side of the card might be matched with a sad expression on the other side.

 ⊃ You can also teach students about the natural outcomes of expected school behaviors using "go-togethers." For example, "completed homework" might be matched with a picture of a good grade or a growing brain.

Notes

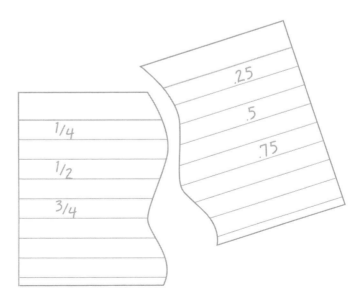

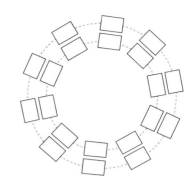

Review Content With Inside/Outside Circles

Standards Links

Mathematics: The student will demonstrate number sense by skip counting by twos, fives and tens.

Science: The student will know the earth's composition and structure (and associated vocabulary).

Overview

Movement activities that can be applied across content areas are often teacher favorites. This strategy fits the bill! Inside/outside circles give students kinesthetic opportunities in which to rehearse critical information and interact with their peers.

What to Do

1. Develop index cards or handouts that contain the information students need to rehearse. In mathematics, this might be a direction to skip count by twos, fives, or tens. In science, cards might include vocabulary and definitions.

2. Divide your class into two even groups. (An extra student can be used as the "caller.")

3. Have one group stand and form a circle facing outward. Give each of the students in the circle an index card or handout.

4. Have the second group stand and form a circle around the first group, facing in. Each student should be facing a partner.

5. Explain that the inside circle of students will pose a question from their cards to their partners in the outside circle. The students on the outside are to answer the question as quickly as possible (but also as accurately as possible). Encourage students to gently correct their partners if an incorrect answer is given.

6. After allowing adequate time, you, or the "caller," say "turn" out loud. The outside circle then moves one person to the right. Everyone should now be paired with a different student than previously.

7. Occasionally direct the inside circle to take a turn turning.

Consider

➲ You can predetermine the questions students will ask, or students can develop their own questions from lecture notes, textbook pages, or handouts.

Notes

Meeting Standards

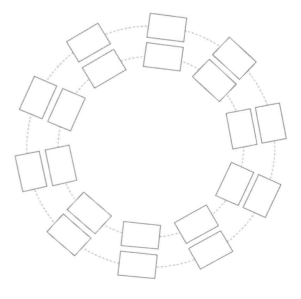

Differentiate Learning With Fold-and-Flips

Standards Links

Writing: The student will write, using conventional grammar; sentence structure; punctuation; capitalization; and spelling.

Mathematics: The student will select and apply appropriate computational techniques to solve a variety of word problems.

Overview

Students learn fastest when the material being presented is at the appropriate instructional level. In diverse classrooms, this means that daily oral language editing exercises, daily math challenges, or other activities may need to be presented at varying levels. This strategy meets this need, while preserving a struggling student's desire for confidentiality.

What to Do

1. Differentiate your daily prompts into two or three levels of difficulty. For example, for editing practice, you might use the following levels:
    - Level 1. john and Marsha went to the library after school
    - Level 2. john and marsha goed to the library after school
    - Level 3. john said to marsh lets go to the library after school

2. Develop one week's worth of prompts in advance.

3. Create fold-and-flips for each student in your class using three pieces of plain or lined paper. Lay one on top of the other, layering them so that the top edge of each sheet is approximately one inch above the top edge of the page underneath it.

4. Fold the papers in half and staple along the folded edge. This will result in a booklet of papers with a cover, plus five one-inch edges showing.

5. Mark the cover "Weekly Fold-and-Flip," and each edge with a day of the week.

Mavi completes her daily fold-and-flip assignment.

6. On the daily pages, write the prompts for each day for the appropriate level for each student.

7. Direct students to complete their daily assignment and hand in the fold-and-flips at the end of the week.

Consider

⮑ Once you've got the hang of making fold-and-flips, you'll know where the prompts appear on the sheets of paper. You may find it quicker and easier to create them on the computer.

⮑ Making fold-and-flips can be a great task for teacher assistants or parent volunteers. A parent with access to a computer might take on the task of inputting the prompts and making a month's worth of fold-and-flips at a time. (Provide a sample so your volunteers see what you want.)

⮑ Because the folded paper provides privacy for students, you can also use these as behavior management systems, self-monitoring systems, or for sending personal notes.

Notes

Make Clear Connections Between Concepts With Learning Links

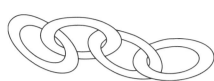

Standards Links

Writing: The student will generate topics and develop ideas for a variety of writing purposes.

Reading: The student will use a full range of strategies to comprehend materials such as fiction, nonfiction, and poetry.

Health: The student will use various strategies for responding to negative peer influences.

Overview

You can make cognitive connections more concrete for students with this strategy. Students physically connect two or more links, while thinking or talking about connections between ideas. In this way, students develop a solid understanding of key relationships.

What to Do

1. Obtain several links per student. Links can be found at the hardware store (metal chain links), from a toy store (colorful plastic ovals), or from a party supply store (plastic bracelets with an opening). Kindergarten and first grade teachers often have plastic links in their math manipulative kits.

2. As you ask a student to make connections between two or more ideas, hold one link in your hand to represent one of the ideas. When the student makes a connection to another idea, hand him or her a link to connect to yours. When the student verbally makes the connection, he or she links to your link. For example, after reading *I Love You the Purplest* by B. M. Joossee (1996), ask students to think of a special person they would like to write about. Tell them to imagine a color that represents that person. When they come up with an idea, they can tell you about it and connect a link to yours.

3. Give the connected learning links to the student to hold during the remainder of the lesson, or have the student connect to links made by other students.

4. If a writing activity follows the discussion, have students place learning links flat on a piece of paper to form a graphic organizer. They can trace the links and write key words inside the traced images as a prewriting activity.

Consider

⟳ If a group of students has formed a long chain of learning links, consider hanging them on display. Add a chart or poster of the ideas discussed, and you have a ready-made review of the material.

⟳ Students can make paper learning links. Simply cut 1" x 6" strips of paper. Have students write their ideas on the strip, loop it through a related idea, and tape the ends together.

Notes

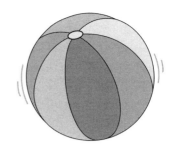

Revitalize Review With Beach-Ball Response

Standards Links

Music: The student will demonstrate understanding of the relationships among music, history, and culture.

Reading: The student will read and respond to written works of differing genres.

Overview

Add spice to review activities with this strategy. It offers kinesthetic activity and unpredictability to awaken students and enhance their retention of information.

What to Do

1. Obtain an inexpensive plastic beach ball (under $1 at most stores).

2. Determine the content you want to review. For example, in music class you might review the characteristics of the musical periods. In literature class you might review the varieties of fiction genres.

3. On each section of the ball, write the key word in permanent marker (e.g., Baroque, Romantic, Classical).

4. Have students stand in a circle, or in two lines facing each other.

5. Tell students that the place where their right hand lands as they catch the ball will dictate the content to which they must respond. For example, they will have to name a characteristic of that period, an example of the genre, etc.

6. Toss the ball to a student. As soon as the student answers, he or she quickly tosses the ball to another student. If a student answers incorrectly, quickly interrupt and provide a correction.

7. Continue at a rapid pace until a thorough review has been accomplished.

Consider

- For younger students it may be more effective to sit on the floor and roll the ball. This will prevent wild throws and lost time spent chasing after wayward beach balls.

- If student skill levels vary widely, allow students one or two free passes. By the time a struggling student has passed twice, enough other students will have responded to the prompts that he or she will have had a fresh review of many ideas.

 At the beginning of the year, when you review classroom rules, label each section of the beach ball with a rule. As a student catches the ball, ask him or her to provide an example of the rule in action.

 Beach balls make great seats for wiggly students! Blow a very small amount of air into the ball. Although it will look uninflated, the air will compress into a thin cushion as the student sits on it. Now the student can move around without being out of his or her seat.

Notes

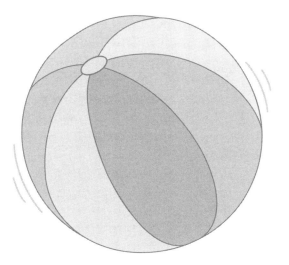

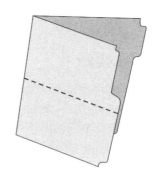

Improve Visual Focus With Work Masks

Standards Links

Reading: The student will make and check predictions about a story by using cover, title, and pictures.

Art: The student will know how ideas and emotions are expressed through visual arts.

 Lifelong Learning: The student will maintain energy and focus over a sustained period of time or activity.

Overview

Many students have difficulty processing visual information. This is especially true when that information is embedded in a crowded field of other information (such as a storybook or text). A simple solution to this problem is the use of masks. Made from file folders, work masks can be designed in several ways to cover a portion of a student worksheet or text page. This allows students to focus on the material needed at the moment.

What to Do

1. Obtain enough file folders to make several work masks available for all your students.

2. Take one file folder and hold it vertically.

3. Using scissors, cut a horizontal line through the front of the folder, approximately in the middle. The folder should now have two flaps.

4. Slide the folder over the page, with one flap over the front and one flap behind the page. Only half of the page will be visible. (Now it's a work mask.)

5. To encourage predictions (and discourage students reading captions), have students place work masks over their pages so that only the picture is showing.

6. After making their predictions, students can reveal the text and read to find out if they are right.

Consider

- ➲ Use work masks to cover worksheets so that students do not feel overwhelmed by a complete page of problems or questions.

- ➲ Cut masks to fit a variety of materials. Try cutting three or four flaps, or making some with horizontal cuts.

- ➲ If any students have individual daily schedules on their desks, consider placing them in work masks. As the periods pass, students slide the mask so that completed periods no longer show, and only remaining periods are visible (or vice versa).

Notes

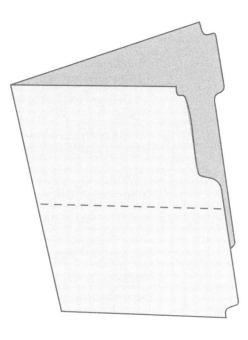

Make Question & Answer Periods More Fun With Fortune Tellers

Standards Links

Mathematics: The student will apply number theory concepts to represent numbers in various ways (e.g., primes, composites, factors, and multiples).

Reading: The student will compare and contrast story elements (characters, settings, events).

Reading: The student will correctly use new vocabulary from literature in other contexts.

Overview

Fortune tellers are finger toys made from folded paper. They can be moved and unfolded to reveal information. Although fortune tellers have been used for years as a toy, they can also be used to teach content in almost any subject area.

Zak learns story elements using a fortune teller.

What to Do

1. Have each student make a fortune teller by following the directions in the sidebar that follows. Many students will have made these in the past and will be able to help those having difficulty.

2. Ask each student to review the materials to be learned and generate eight content questions and answers. In math, this might include eight squared numbers and their square roots. In literature, students might develop eight questions and answers about the story they read as a class.

3. Direct students to write their questions on the inside flaps of the fortune teller, with the corresponding answers underneath the flaps.

4. On the top of the fortune teller, students can print the numbers 1, 2, 3, and 4, write four colors (red, yellow, blue, green), four spelling words, or a four-word statement, such as "I love math facts."

5. When all the students have completed their fortune tellers, ask them to work with a partner. Each student takes a turn manipulating the fortune teller while the partner chooses and answers a question.

Making a Fortune Teller

Step 1. Start with a square piece of paper (8½" x 8½" works well).

Step 2. Fold the square in half diagonally to make a triangle.

Step 3. Fold the resulting triangle in half vertically to make a smaller triangle.

Step 4. Open up the paper to the original square.

Step 5. Take each corner and fold it in to meet the center of the square, forming a smaller square when finished.

Step 6. Flip the square over so that the smooth surface is on top.

Step 7. Repeat Step 5.

Step 8. Fold the square in half horizontally, creasing the fold, and then open it back up.

Step 9. Fold the square in half vertically, creasing the fold, and then open it back up. You now have a blank fortune teller!

Consider

- ⟳ Fortune tellers can be fun homework assignments. Students can take them home to review material learned in school or use them to study for a test.

- ⟳ Very young children may have difficulty folding the fortune tellers. For these students, you may wish to make the fortune tellers ahead of time.

 ⟳ Use fortune tellers to make your reward system more unpredictable and motivating. Instead of placing questions and answers on the flaps, place the numbers 1 through 8 on the top flaps, with a different reward under each.

Notes

Powerful Review With Pegboards

Standards Links

Mathematics: The student will reproduce, extend, create, and describe patterns and sequences using a variety of materials.

Social Studies: The student will differentiate between historical fact and folklore.

 Lifelong Learning: The student will use structured and discretionary time in appropriate ways.

Overview

This hands-on strategy has almost endless possibilities in classrooms. By using colored pegs, students can record their responses to a variety of questions, problems, or activities on pegboards. As soon as students finish the task, the pegboard can be refitted for another task, making them a reusable, long-lasting instructional tool.

Kengy uses a pegboard to answer questions.

What to Do

1. Obtain a pegboard and multicolored pegs from your local teacher store or toy store.

2. Develop a legend for the colored pegs. For example:
   True = Green
   False = Red
   Or:
   Character = Blue
   Setting = Green
   Action = Red

3. Develop a worksheet for the standard you are addressing. The worksheet could be a list of true/false questions or a study of story elements and a comprehension review including several sentences from a story.

4. Tape the worksheet to the pegboard so that the statements or sentences line up with the holes on the board, leaving one column of holes uncovered. (Depending on the size of your pegboard, you many need to adjust the font size and line space on your word processing software.)

5. Provide the students with several pegs of the necessary colors. Direct them to place a colored peg in the hole that corresponds to the

statement or sentence. In a true/false activity, for example, the student should place a green peg in the hole next to Statement 1 if they believe the statement is true. If analyzing story elements, the student would place a green peg next to any lines of the story that contain words that indicate or describe the setting.

Consider

 ⟳ Avoid the worksheets altogether and use the pegboards for building mathematical arrays, geometric shapes, one-to-one correspondence, basic math fact manipulatives, etc.

⟳ Use the pegboard to develop daily schedules for the class or for individual students. To do this, print a list of the activities of the school day. Color-code each of the subject areas (e.g., green = science). Have students review the schedule in the morning, adding the colored pegs to each line as they do so. When the activity is finished, students remove the peg.

Notes

111

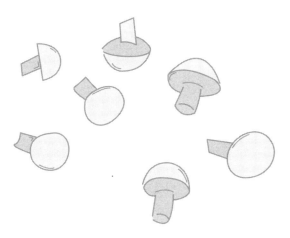

Increase Proficiency With "Name That Number"

12

Standards Links

Mathematics: The student will demonstrate proficiency with basic addition, subtraction, multiplication, and division facts without the use of a calculator.

Mathematics: The student will construct, use, and explain procedures used in problem-solving situations.

Overview

Math experts tell us that children must learn to use numbers in a flexible way, seeing a variety of solutions instead of just one. "Name That Number" encourages this, while addressing the various levels of math skill in the diverse classroom.

What to Do

1. Make and cut two copies of Reproducible 5.8, *"Name That Number" Cards* for each student. (Regular playing cards can also be used if available.)

2. Copy Reproducible 5.8 onto transparency film and cut these into individual cards. Use this set to demonstrate the game on the overhead projector.

3. Ask students to find a partner, and give each pair of students a set of cards.

4. Have students watch as you demonstrate "Name That Number" on the overhead projector.

5. Place one card face up as shown in *Figure 5.5*, with five additional cards face up below it. The top card is the target number.

Figure 5.5: The "Name That Number" layout.

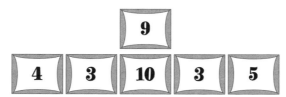

6. Use any of the five cards in the row to match the target number. This may mean adding two or more, subtracting, multiplying, dividing, or

any combination of these approaches. Higher level thinkers may decide to use negative numbers. As the match is made, the player must talk through the math process out loud.

7. The player keeps any of the cards he or she uses to match the target number until the end of the game.

8. If the second player thought of a different way to play the hand, he or she can show the partner, but does not keep the cards.

9. When the first player is finished, the second player draws a new target card and replaces the lower cards that have been taken (unused cards remain).

10. Players take turns until cards run out. Whoever has the most cards wins!

Consider

⊃ For a noncompetitive approach, have partners work together to see how many cards they can collect by the end of the game.

⊃ "Name That Number" can be played alone. Try "Name That Number" during individual work times, or for students who have finished work ahead of their peers.

⊃ Suggest "Name That Number" as a fun homework assignment for review of math facts and exploration of higher level mathematical thinking.

This strategy has been adapted with permission from McGraw Hill, (2002) *Everyday Mathematics: Student Reference Book Fifth Grade.*

Notes

Cross-Discipline Writing and Note-Taking With Model Notebooks

Standards Links

Writing: The student will use writing as a tool for learning in all subjects (making lists, paraphrasing, summarizing, synthesizing).

Lifelong Learning: The student will apply organizational and study skills across the content areas.

Overview

This is an excellent method for students to check that they have correctly recorded key information from lectures. In addition, it provides you with a tool to assess how thoroughly students have grasped the concept or information you have taught.

What to Do

1. Contact your local print shop or a printer who works with your school district. Ask for a ream of lined, three-part carbonless paper. Each sheet has a white top leaf, and yellow and pink tear sheets. (This is the type of paper used for many school forms.)

2. At the beginning of the class or lecture, give three-part paper to your strongest note-taker. Ask him or her to take notes on the white page, remembering to place the date in the top right-hand corner.

3. At the end of the lecture, ask the note-taker to keep the white page for his or her own notebook and hand in the pink and yellow pages.

4. Three-hole punch the yellow page and place it in a three-ring binder, labeled as "Model Notebook."

5. Encourage students to check their own notes against the model notebook to determine if they captured the key information. (This is especially helpful for students who have been absent.)

6. From time to time, glance through the model notebook to see if students seem to understand the key concepts. If not, reteach the material.

7. The pink page can be used in two ways:
   - Give the pink page to a student who has an excused absence. This will save peers from having to hand over their notes, perhaps never to see them again.

- If there is a student with a disability who cannot simultaneously take notes and listen effectively, the pink page can be given to him or her. This will alleviate the frustration of trying to do both, and encourage him or her to focus on listening and comprehending.

Consider

➲ Vary who you choose to be the note-taker for the model notebook. Generally, students who take on this task vastly improve their note-taking skills.

➲ If you decide to give the pink page to a struggling student (as in Step 7), suggest that the student continue to keep a notebook on the desk. This decreases the likelihood that the student will be ostracized for being different and encourages the student to continue working on note-taking skills.

Notes

Touchy Subjects: Learning With Labelmakers

6 × 6 = 36 7 × 7 = 49

Standards Links

Writing: The student will use correct spelling for frequently used words.

Mathematics: The student will recognize and write numerals 0–100.

Lifelong Learning: The student will use a variety of strategies and tools to organize materials.

Overview

This strategy uses a label-making device to produce plastic, raised strips of words and numbers. Both the input of information into the labelmaker and the output provide intense, tactile experience and review opportunities.

Mavi learns multiplication with a labelmaker.

What to Do

1. Obtain labelmakers and labeling tapes from the office supply section of your local store.

2. Show students how to turn the top dial to the desired letter or number, and then squeeze the handle to imprint the letter.

3. Provide students with a list of key information.

4. Direct students to squeeze the handle and imprint the information onto the tape. For example, the student might imprint spelling words, vocabulary words, state capitals, equivalents, etc.

5. After the tapes have been imprinted, ask students to peel off the plastic backing and adhere the labels to sheets of heavy paper or large index cards.

6. When it is time to review the material, have students run their fingers over the labels as they rehearse the information aloud.

Consider

➲ If the information is adhered to index cards, store the cards in a small box. Encourage students to access these in order to rehearse the information.

➲ Post the finished labels along the wall where students typically line up to leave the room. As they are waiting to be dismissed, they can touch and review the information.

 ➲ Use this strategy to make individual student schedules. The tactile nature of the label appeals to many struggling students.

 ➲ Direct students to use labelmakers for key homework assignments. These can be adhered directly onto students' assignment notebooks.

Notes

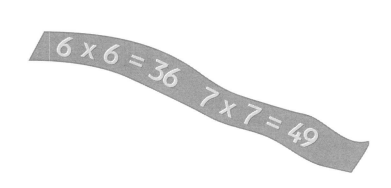

Diversify Instruction With Music Videos

Standards Links

Science: The student will understand the various forms of energy.

Technology: The student will demonstrate a basic understanding of computer theory.

Overview

Brain research suggests that music, when linked to specific content, is a very powerful force in retention. This musical strategy encourages students to make personal meaning of new information. It results in an excellent source of review materials.

What to Do

1. After your initial introduction of material, determine the key knowledge that students need to master. Make an outline or list of the key points.

2. Place students into groups of 4 – 6.

3. Explain that they will work in their groups to write and produce a music video covering the key points of the material.

4. Direct students to choose a familiar tune and change the words to include the key points. (This will save a great deal of time and frustration.) Share examples of age-appropriate tunes that everyone might know.

5. Make sure students are aware of the time frame you allot. This can vary tremendously based on the age of your students and the difficulty of the content. Generally, 20 – 45 minutes is sufficient.

6. When students are ready to perform, videotape each presentation. Label the videos according to the content covered in the song.

7. Set aside a library shelf for the music videos. Allow students to check them out for home review and study. Show the videos to the whole class as a component of review lessons or prior to tests on the material.

Consider

- ⟳ If a video camera is not available, use a cassette tape recorder.

- ⟳ Consult your school district policy on photographing and videotaping students. If necessary, obtain permission slips from parents.

- ⟳ This strategy can be used with individual students as well. It is especially effective for students who are musically talented or who have a strong musical intelligence. In these cases, consider offering students the option of developing their own music, rather than using a familiar tune.

Notes

Foster Independent Decision-Making With Color Dots

Standards Links

Social Studies: The student will understand that people in the United States and Canada can influence the action and decisions of their governments through voting.

Writing: The student will generate writing topics and develop ideas using prewriting techniques.

Lifelong Learning: The student will act independently based on knowledge of personal needs and preferences.

Overview

Many students struggle with prioritizing and choice-making. These skills affect their thinking and decision-making across the content areas. This is a highly visual and tactile strategy that makes abstract thoughts more concrete.

What to Do

1. Ask the school office for a supply of colored adhesive dots (the type used to label folders).

2. When students have a task that requires them to prioritize and make choices, furnish them with a sheet of color dots.

3. Direct students to use their dots as "votes." For example, to write an essay, students need to choose one topic from a brainstorm list of a dozen ideas. They review the list once. For every idea that appeals to them, they stick a dot beside it. After the first review, direct them to review the dotted items and place another dot next to the items that are strong favorites. Continue as necessary, until one topic has the most dots.

4. For a higher level approach, develop a legend for color-coding. Students then use the legend to consider several variables in their decision-making processes. For example, in a social studies or civics lesson, colors might represent the following:

    Quick solution = Red

    No-cost solution = Green

    Environmentally-friendly solution = Yellow

    Long-lasting solution = Blue

Consider

○ Use color dots as a class-wide approach to voting. Write the items to be voted on on a chart pad. Direct students to come up, a few at a time, and vote with their dots.

○ Suggest that students use the color dot strategy when studying for a test. Direct them to place dots next to the notes they feel are most critical to study. (Some struggling students may need help determining where to place their dots.)

Notes

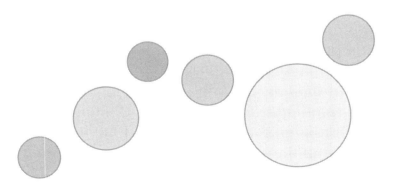

Teach Time Lines, Methods, and Processes With Kinesthetic Sequencing

Standards Links

Social Studies: The student will know how to construct time lines using months, years, decades, and centuries.

Mathematics: The student will know, use, and describe the advantages and disadvantages of a variety of problem-solving sequences.

Science: The student will know, use, and describe the advantages and disadvantages of a chosen scientific method.

Overview

You can engage students in kinesthetic responses to content by asking them to physically demonstrate a sequence. By doing so, abstract sequences become more concrete and understandable.

What to Do

1. Determine the content to be sequenced and write each step of the sequence on a separate index card. In a history lesson, this may be a list of important events. In math or science, this may be the steps in a problem-solving process.

2. Distribute the index cards to students.

3. Direct students to bring their cards to the front of the room and line up, holding their cards facing out so that their peers can read them.

4. Once in place, direct students to rearrange themselves according to the correct sequence.

5. Ask one or more students to judge whether the sequence is correct.

Consider

⤷ Students in wheelchairs can participate, too. If they are not independently mobile, ask peers to assist in wheeling them up to the line and into the correct places.

⤷ Use this strategy to indicate levels of interest or agreement on a subject or statement. Ask students to stand along an imaginary continuum, with the far right indicating strong agreement, the center being neutral, and the far left indicating strong disagreement.

Notes

Increase the Participation of *All* Your Students With "Numbered Heads Together"

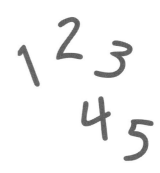

Standards Links

Mathematics: The student will represent and use numbers in a variety of equivalent forms.

Science: The student will investigate and understand how plants interact with their nonliving environment.

Reading: The student will use a full range of strategies to comprehend fiction and nonfiction.

Overview

Struggling students are usually hesitant to volunteer to answer questions during large group instruction. Their participation tends to decrease as they experience the embarrassment of being wrong in front of the class. When they stop volunteering, they may also stop trying to figure out the answer, even for themselves. Comprehension decreases, leading to low outcomes on standards. "Numbered Heads Together" (Kagan 1994) is a supportive, nonthreatening approach that increases participation of all students in the class, leading to improved comprehension for all.

What to Do

1. Divide the class into groups of four or five. Assign every student in the group a number, from one to five. (In a class of 30 students, there should be six students who are "ones," six who are "twos," etc.)

2. Explain that all students will work together to learn the answers to the questions. When you say "numbered heads together," they are to turn to their groups and do two things. First, they are to develop the best possible answer to the question posed. Second, they are to make sure that everyone can recite and explain the answer.

3. On the board, write the directions as follows:
   - Turn to and work with your group.
   - Develop the best answer to the question.
   - Make sure everyone knows the answer.

4. Present the class with a question you want all of them to be able to answer. For example, in science you might ask, "What role does the sun

play in the process of photosynthesis?" In mathematics, the question might be: "What are three different ways to name the distance of three feet?"

5. After you pose the question, say "numbered heads together." Check to see that students are turning to their groups to work out the answer.

6. After allowing sufficient time for the task, inform students that time is up. Repeat the original question and then, at random, call on a number from one to five. Say "All the number twos who know the answer, please raise your hand." Choose someone to answer the question. If students answer incorrectly, gently correct them and reteach the concept during an upcoming lesson.

7. The more often you use this strategy, the more often students will raise their hands to indicate that they have the answers. Students begin to realize that they need to make sure everyone in the group really does know and understand the answer, and that it will be obvious if their group did not fully complete the task.

Consider

⟳ Arrange groups heterogeneously, so that no one group is overwhelmed with struggling students or dominated by gifted students.

⟳ As a reverse twist on this strategy, ask students to work in groups to develop questions about areas of the content that are still unclear. After a few minutes have passed, ask for "group questions." This provides struggling students with an anonymous outlet for questions about things they don't understand, and provides you with a better sense of areas that need to be covered in more depth.

Notes

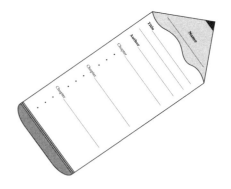

Encourage Active Reading With Bullet Bookmarks

Standards Links

Reading: The student will use a variety of strategies to understand text.

Writing: The student will use a variety of writing strategies to gather and organize information.

Overview

Succinct summarization is a skill critical to comprehension, analysis, and retention. Bullet bookmarks help students summarize their reading as they move from chapter to chapter, capturing the essence of each section on an ever-present bookmark.

What to Do

1. Copy Reproducible 5.9, *Pencil Bookmark* and cut out the bookmarks, making one for each student.

2. Fold the bookmark in half, backward, along the fold line.

3. Direct students to put their names, book titles, and authors at the top of their bookmarks.

4. Explain that summarizing as they read will make it easier to retain key information and review prior to tests. Direct them to jot down three bullets as they read each chapter.

5. After students fill the first side, direct them to flip the bookmark over and continue on the second side, eventually using the back if necessary.

Consider

⮑ Laminate the bookmarks and have students record their notes using wipe-off markers. Now you can use the bookmarks over and over.

⮑ Instead of three general ideas from the chapter, students can record points about the characters, settings, or any other focus of your teaching.

⮑ To ensure that students use these bookmarks as intended, consider requiring them to turn them in at the end of the book or unit. Bookmarks can become an assignment that receives credit toward the grade.

Notes

127

Chapter 6

Making the Most
of Each Strategy

A great strategy is one that is simple and effective and generalizes easily across content areas. In order to make the most of each of the strategies presented in this book, I encourage you to generalize their use beyond the proposed content standards. To help you do that, I'd like to offer one more strategy. However, this time I will present the strategy without the standards links, then show the process you can follow to develop variations and generalizations across content areas. Turn to the next page for the final strategy.

Monitor Learning With Bead Counters

Overview

A bead counter is a hand-held device that allows students to concretely track progress or process by sliding beads along a piece of string. The visual and tactile input is strong, and students enjoy the sense of accomplishment they receive from moving the beads.

What to Do

1. Gather one green, one yellow, and one red bead of similar size and shape. The hole in the beads should be large enough to accommodate two strands of yarn.

2. Cut an 18-inch piece of blue yarn and fold it in half. Tie a knot in the folded end of the yarn, large enough so that the beads will not slip past.

3. Lay the yarn on the table, with the knot at the top. Separate the two hanging strands by a few inches, pushing one to the left and one to the right.

4. Using the green bead, thread the right strand of yarn through the bead, from right to left. Then thread the left strand of yarn through the same bead, but from left to right. Pull both strands so that the bead is pushed up against the top knot.

5. Using the yellow bead, repeat Step 4.

6. Using the red bead, repeat Step 4.

7. Pick up both strands of yarn and tie a knot approximately 1 – 2 inches below the red bead. The knot should be large enough so that beads cannot slip past.

8. You now have a bead counter! Beads can be slid up and down the yarn strands to track progress. Because of the resistance of the crossed yarn strands, the bead will stay in place when it is pushed up or down. This makes it easy for students to know exactly where they stand.

My first use of bead counters was in conjunction with a writing lesson. Students were learning that every paragraph needed a beginning, middle, and end. I chose green, yellow, and red to represent the components of the paragraph. I chose blue yarn because I would later introduce blue as the color that represents writing transitions. As students analyzed well-written paragraphs, they were to move the green bead up when they found the beginning, the yellow when they found the middle, and the red when they found the ending. We later used the bead counters as students wrote their own paragraphs, moving the beads to show that all three components were present.

The bead counters were so effective with students, that I knew I had latched onto an idea that might have greater uses. Let's take a look to see how I went about the process of generalizing this strategy to other content standards (and how you can, too!).

To generate variations and generalizations, begin with Reproducible 6.1, *Making the Most of the Strategy*. Place the name of the strategy in the center of the graphic organizer. Brainstorm ideas that fit into each of the content areas and write them in the appropriate places. You'll see from the example in *Figure 6.1* that the ideas should be standards-driven but need not include the exact, entire wording of the standard. Once you have filled in all your ideas, record necessary adaptations of the main strategy to the side of the arrow. For example, if using bead counters for one-to-one correspondence in math, it is necessary to have at least 10 beads, and they can be all the same color.

Using this process, I found that bead counters generalize to all content areas. However, there are certain strategies that might apply to several standards links, but within only one or two content areas. Of course, these are still valuable, as long as they lead to student learning! If you have found a few connections for a strategy but want to develop more, ask a colleague to brainstorm with you. Many of the best variations come from a quick, lively discussion among colleagues over lunch. You will find that the time and effort put into developing a strategy reaps expanded rewards for your students.

Figure 6.1: An example of how to make the most of the beadcounter strategy.

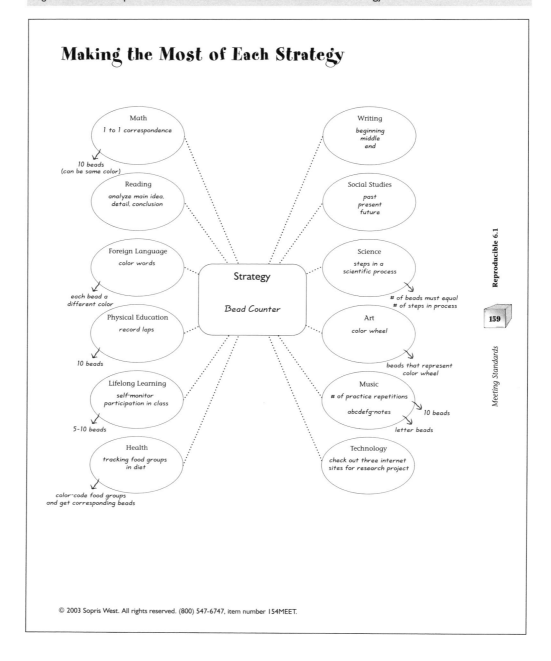

Making the Most of Each Strategy

© 2003 Sopris West. All rights reserved. (800) 547-6747, item number 154MEET.

Reproducibles

Student Learning Style Observation

Student Name _____ Grade _____ Date _____

Teacher _____

Check the behaviors that you observe the student exhibiting frequently.

Visual

- ❑ Taking copious notes
- ❑ Drawing or doodling
- ❑ Wanting to look at the pictures accompanying text
- ❑ Needing eye contact to listen well
- ❑ Choosing visual tasks, such as reading
- ❑ Closely examining objects and pictures
- ❑ Commenting on the visual aspects of something

Auditory

- ❑ Choosing to listen to audiotapes
- ❑ Following verbal directions while not appearing to be listening
- ❑ Showing a preference for music or singing
- ❑ Showing an interest in oral discussions
- ❑ Reading aloud to self
- ❑ Sounding out words
- ❑ Talking to self

Tactile

- ❑ Touching objects on shelves
- ❑ Fiddling with items in desk
- ❑ Carrying small objects around in hand
- ❑ Choosing to work with manipulatives whenever possible
- ❑ Grabbing items
- ❑ Playing with pencils and pens

Kinesthetic

- ❑ Walking around the room
- ❑ Standing while working at desk
- ❑ Jumping out of seat
- ❑ Using body movements for expression
- ❑ Enjoying physical education and other movement opportunities
- ❑ Volunteering to demonstrate or run errands
- ❑ Acting and playing roles

Reproducible 3.1

Meeting Standards

135

© 2003 Sopris West. All rights reserved. (800) 547-6747, item number I54MEET. Reprinted with permission of Beninghof, A.

Student Information Form

Student Name _____   Grade _____   Date _____

Teacher _____

Gather and analyze information about the student. Be sure to include student strengths and needs.

Standardized Test Scores

Classroom Assessments (e.g., informal reading inventories, work samples, teacher-made tests)

Anecdotal Information

Learning Styles

© 2003 Sopris West. All rights reserved. (800) 547-6747, item number 154MEET.

Standards-Based Strategies for Individual Students

Student Name _____   Grade _____   Date _____

Teacher(s) _____

Student Information

Areas of Strength	Learning Styles	Areas of Need

Standards of Focus

Content Area _____   Content Area _____

Standard	Standard
Supportive Strategies	Supportive Strategies

Evaluation Plan

Process	Date(s)	Person(s) Responsible

Reproducible 3.3

137

© 2003 Sopris West. All rights reserved. (800) 547-6747, item number 154MEET.

Standards-Based Strategies for Groups

Group _____

Teacher(s) _____ Grade _____ Date _____

Group Information

Group Strengths	Group Learning Style	Group Needs

Standards of Focus

Area _____ Area _____

Standard	Standard

Supportive Strategies	Supportive Strategies

Evaluation Plan

Process	Date(s)	Person(s) Responsible

© 2003 Sopris West. All rights reserved. (800) 547-6747, item number 154MEET.

Group Learning Style Profile

Group _____

Teacher_____ Date _____

Write the names of students in the quadrant which most represents their dominant learning style.

Visual _____

Auditory _____

Tactile _____

Kinesthetic _____

Reproducible 3.5

139

Meeting Standards

© 2003 Sopris West. All rights reserved. (800) 547-6747, item number 154MEET.

Standards-Based Home Strategies

Student Name _____   Grade _____   Date _____

Teacher(s) _____

Standard	Things to try at home
Your child is struggling with these standards in school.	You may want to try these things at home to help your child. Please contact your child's teacher if you have any questions.

© 2003 Sopris West. All rights reserved. (800) 547-6747, item number 154MEET.

Larry's "Laptop" Keyboard

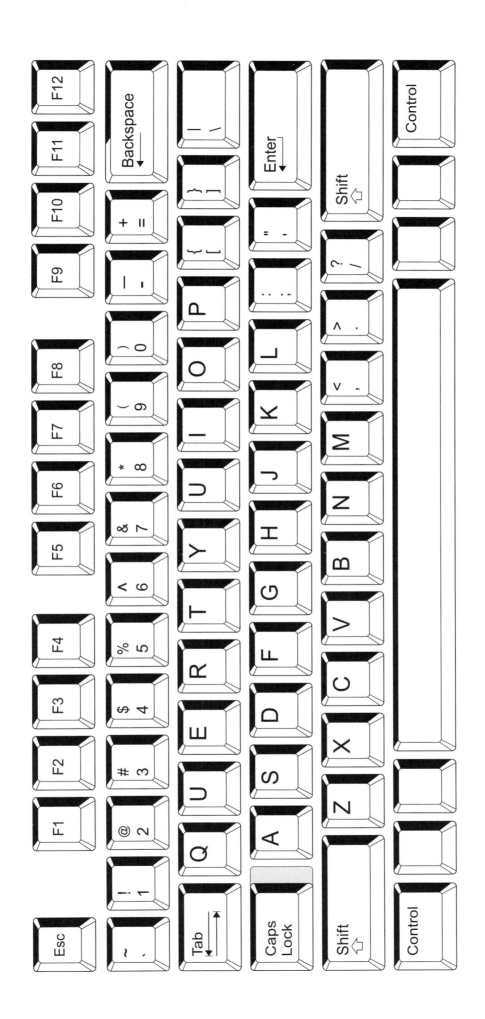

© 2003 Sopris West. All rights reserved. (800) 547-6747, item number 154MEET.

Meeting Standards

141

Reproducible 5.1

Story Elements Graphic Organizer

Student Name _____ Date _____

Title _____

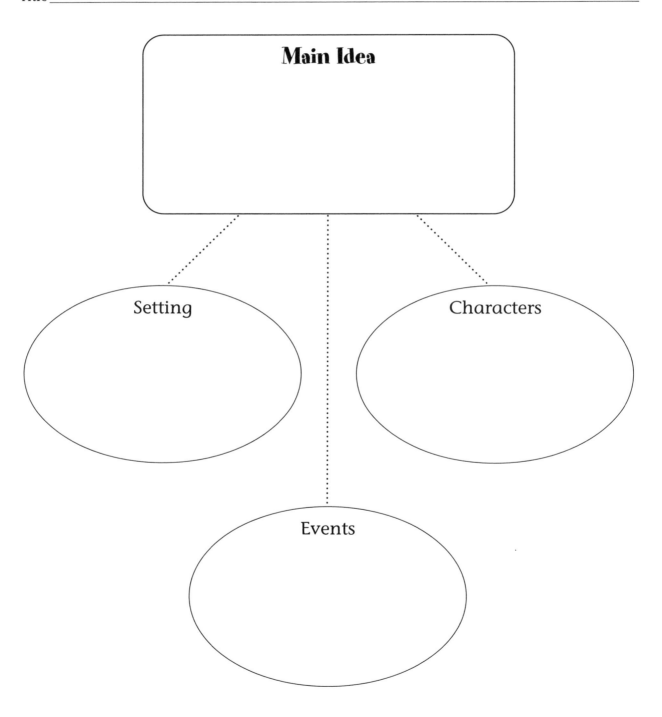

Reproducible 5.2a

142

Meeting Standards

© 2003 Sopris West. All rights reserved. (800) 547-6747, item number 154MEET.

Process/Sequence Graphic Organizer

Student Name _____   Date _____

Topic/Title _____

Reproducible 5.2b

143

Meeting Standards

© 2003 Sopris West. All rights reserved. (800) 547-6747, item number 154MEET.

Cause & Effect Graphic Organizer

Student Name _____   Date _____

Title/Topic _____

Cause		Effect
	→	
	→	
	→	
	→	
	→	

Reproducible 5.2c

144

Meeting Standards

© 2003 Sopris West. All rights reserved. (800) 547-6747, item number 154MEET.

Main Idea/Supporting Details

Student Name _____   Date _____

Title/Topic _____

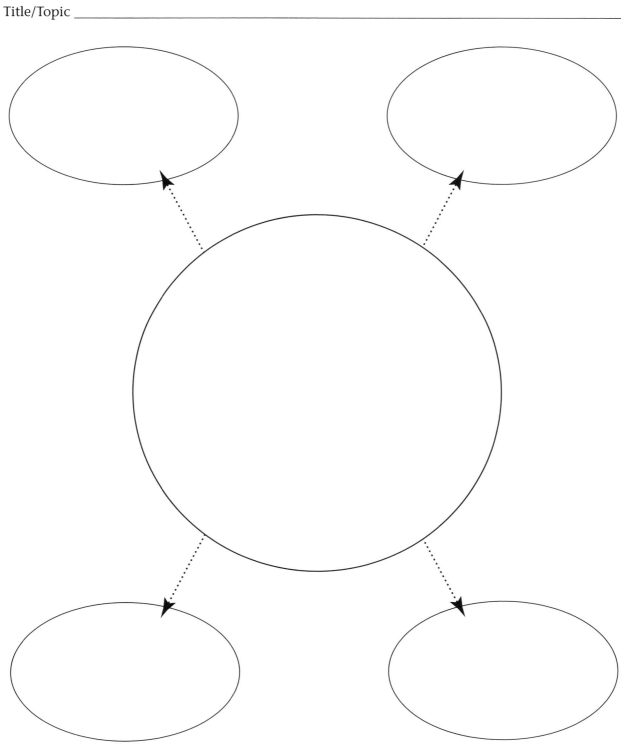

Reproducible 5.2d

145

Meeting Standards

© 2003 Sopris West. All rights reserved. (800) 547-6747, item number 154MEET.

Venn Diagram

Student Name _____ Date _____

Title/Topic _____

Reproducible 5.2e

Meeting Standards

146

© 2003 Sopris West. All rights reserved. (800) 547-6747, item number 154MEET.

Note-Taking Quilt

Student Name _____   Date _____

Title/Topic _____

147

Meeting Standards

© 2003 Sopris West. All rights reserved. (800) 547-6747, item number 154MEET.

Quick and Simple Instructions for Making an "I Spy" Quilt

1. Collect a wide variety of novelty fabric scraps (fabric with obvious characters and pictures of recognizable objects, e.g., car, book, house).

2. Determine the desired size of the finished quilt. A nice size for classroom use is 3' x 4'.

3. Cut the fabric scraps into 3¼-inch squares, with each square capturing a picture. You will need a total of 192 squares. If desired, you can alternate novelty squares with squares of solid fabric (96 of each).

4. For 3' x 4' quilt, sew 12 squares together in a horizontal strip, maintaining a ¼-inch seam between each square.

5. Continue to sew strips of equal length, until you have 16 strips.

6. When finished with all strips, sew them together vertically, again maintaining a ¼-inch seam.

7. Snip loose threads.

8. Add a soft fabric backing of the same size as the finished quilt and bind together the edges of the top and back.

© 2003 Sopris West. All rights reserved. (800) 547-6747, item number 154MEET.

My Quilt

Student Name _____   Date _____

1. Read a direction.

2. Find the correct square.

3. Write the number of the direction in that square.

4. Continue to the end of the directions.

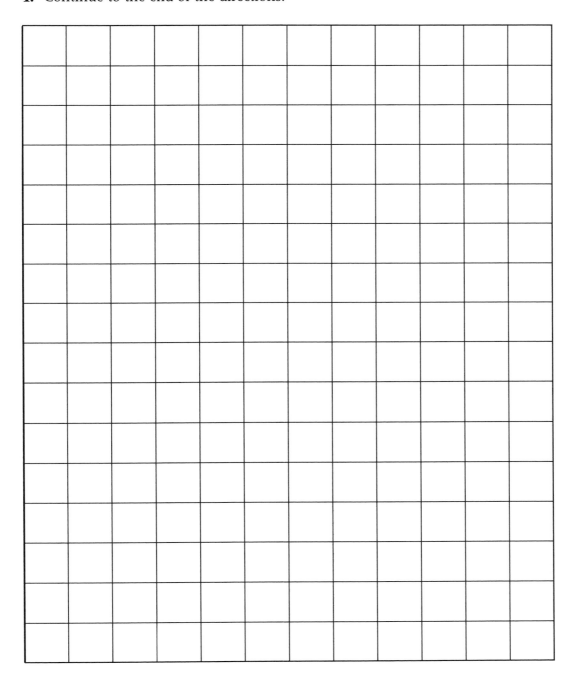

© 2003 Sopris West. All rights reserved. (800) 547-6747, item number I54MEET.

Reproducible 5.4b

149

Meeting Standards

Match 'Em Up Daily Activities

Subjects

Reproducible 5.5a

Meeting Standards

150

Art

Geography

History

Math

$$1+1=2$$

Music

Physical Education

Reading

© 2003 Sopris West. All rights reserved. (800) 547-6747, item number I54MEET.

Match 'Em Up Daily Activities

Science

Social Studies

Spelling

c-a-t

Writing

Other Activities

Arrival

Assembly

Break Time

Reproducible 5.5b

151

Meeting Standards

© 2003 Sopris West. All rights reserved. (800) 547-6747, item number 154MEET.

Match 'Em Up Daily Activities

Bus

Class Meeting

Computers

Dismissal

Field Trip

Free Time

Health Room

Home

Reproducible 5.5c

Meeting Standards

© 2003 Sopris West. All rights reserved. (800) 547-6747, item number 154MEET.

Match 'Em Up Daily Activities

Independent Work

Library

Lunch

Snack

Special Event

© 2003 Sopris West. All rights reserved. (800) 547-6747, item number I54MEET.

Match 'Em Up Daily Schedule

Student Name _____   Date _____

Time	Activity

© 2003 Sopris West. All rights reserved. (800) 547-6747, item number 154MEET.

Sign and Spell

Student Name _____   Date _____

Directions: Write and spell your spelling words three times.

Word				Sign

Reproducible 5.6

155

Meeting Standards

© 2003 Sopris West. All rights reserved. (800) 547-6747, item number 154MEET.

Self-Monitoring Chart

Student Name _____ Dates _____ Task _____

Directions: Color in the corresponding number of squares.

Reproducible 5.7

156

Meeting Standards

	Monday	Tuesday	Wednesday	Thursday	Friday
20					
19					
18					
17					
16					
15					
14					
13					
12					
11					
10					
9					
8					
7					
6					
5					
4					
3					
2					
1					

© 2003 Sopris West. All rights reserved. (800) 547-6747, item number 154MEET.

"Name That Number" Cards

1	2	3	4
5	6	7	8
9	10	11	12
1	2	3	4
5	6	7	8
9	10	11	12

© 2003 Sopris West. All rights reserved. (800) 547-6747, item number 154MEET.

Pencil Bookmark

Reproducible 5.9

158

Meeting Standards

Name
_____

Title_____

_____

Author_____

Chapter_____

•

•

•

Chapter_____

•

•

•

Chapter_____

•

•

•

Name
_____

Chapter_____

•

•

•

Chapter_____   _____

•

•

•

Chapter_____

•

•

•

Chapter_____

•

•

•

© 2003 Sopris West. All rights reserved. (800) 547-6747, item number 154MEET.

Making the Most of Each Strategy

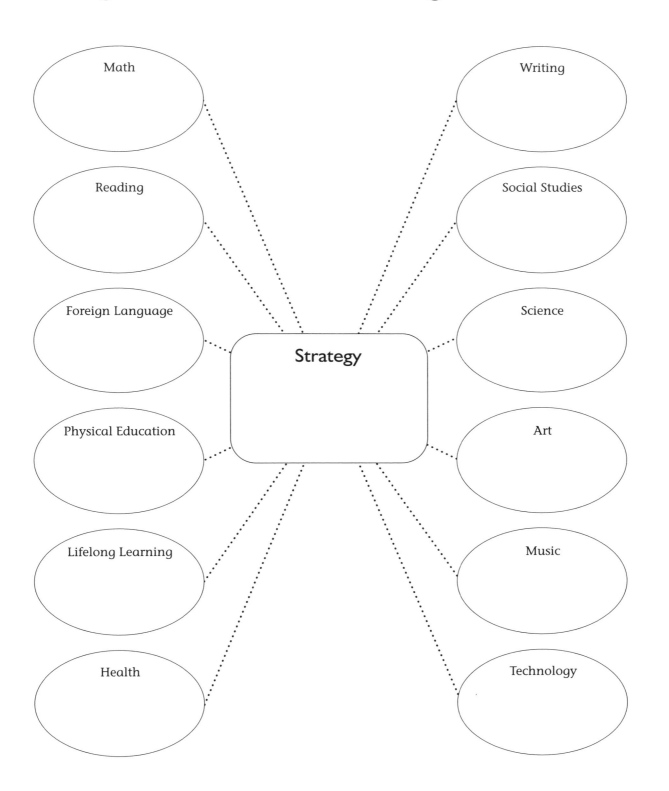

Math

Reading

Foreign Language

Physical Education

Lifelong Learning

Health

Strategy

Writing

Social Studies

Science

Art

Music

Technology

© 2003 Sopris West. All rights reserved. (800) 547-6747, item number 154MEET.

Reproducible 6.1

159

Meeting Standards

Proposed Standards from National Organizations

Arts

Consortium of National Arts Education Associations (1994) *National standards for arts education: What students should know and be able to do in the arts.* Reston, VA: Music Educators National Conference.

Civics, Geography, and History

Center for Civic Education (1994) *National standards for civics and government.* Calabasas, CA: Author.

Geography Education Standards Project (1994) *Geography for life: National geography standards.* Washington, D.C.: National Geographic Research and Exploration.

National Council for Social Studies (1994) *Expectations of excellence: Curriculum standards for social studies.* Waldorf, MD: Author.

Foreign Language

National Standards for Foreign Language Education Project (1999) *Standards for foreign language learning in the 21st century.* Yonkers, NY: American Council on the Teaching of Foreign Languages.

Health

Joint Committee on National Health Education Standards (1995). *National health education standards: Achieving health literacy for all students.* Reston, VA: American Association for Health Education.

Language Arts

National Council of Teachers of English and the International Reading Association (1996) *Standards for the english language arts.* Urbana, IL: National Council of Teachers of English.

National Communication Association (1998) *The speaking, listening and media literacy standards and competency statements for K through 12 education.* Annandale, VA: Author.

Mathematics

National Council of Teachers of Mathematics (2000) *Principles and standards for school mathematics.* Reston, VA: Author.

Physical Education

National Association for Sport and Physical Education (1995) *Moving into the future, national standards for physical education: A guide to content and assessment.* Reston, VA: Author.

Science and Technology

International Technology Education Association (2000) *Standards for technology literacy: Content for the study of technology.* Reston, VA: Author.

National Research Council (1996) *National science education standards.* Washington, D.C.: National Academy Press.

Appendix B

Access Skills

The following list will help you determine an area of focus for a student who needs to improve lifelong learning skills.

Communication and Basic Language

- ⟳ Attending
- ⟳ Listening
- ⟳ Interpreting meaning
- ⟳ Responding to others
- ⟳ Expressing self
- ⟳ Gaining/maintaining attention
- ⟳ Following and giving directions
- ⟳ Consistently attaching meaning to symbol
- ⟳ Acknowledging and honoring others' statements of needs, wants, and feeling
- ⟳ Using alternative communication methods
- ⟳ Other:

Decision-Making and Problem-Solving

- ⟳ Using conflict resolution
- ⟳ Self-initiating activities, tasks, assignments, etc.
- ⟳ Setting goals to plan for action
- ⟳ Using discretionary time in appropriate ways
- ⟳ Self-monitoring behavior and time

- ⊃ Advocating for self and needs
- ⊃ Persuading others
- ⊃ Indicating understanding of cause/effect
- ⊃ Other:

Organization

- ⊃ Demonstrating time management skills
- ⊃ Gaining and applying study skills and learning strategies for managing self
- ⊃ Self-monitoring
- ⊃ Using and organizing materials appropriately
- ⊃ Sequencing events to plan
- ⊃ Identifying and accessing resources
- ⊃ Other:

Inter/Intrapersonal

- ⊃ Demonstrating socially acceptable behaviors
- ⊃ Demonstrating appropriate behavior to the group
- ⊃ Cooperatively working with others in group situation
- ⊃ Demonstrating social amenities
- ⊃ Gaining/maintaining interest/leisure skills
- ⊃ Other:

Self-Advocacy/Self-Determination

- ⊃ Asking for and/or accepting peer support
- ⊃ Assessing situations for equal access and asking for adjustments when appropriate
- ⊃ Expressing physical needs
- ⊃ Expressing personal preferences and choices
- ⊃ Expressing simple feeling states
- ⊃ Expressing other feeling states
- ⊃ Expressing understanding of difference
- ⊃ Describing personal learning limitations
- ⊃ Negotiating adjustments
- ⊃ Evaluating effectiveness of a variety of learning strategies and making adjustments as needed
- ⊃ Developing and maintaining a supportive network

- Acting independently based on knowledge of personal needs and preferences
- Advocating for others as well as issues and ideas
- Using self-regulation techniques
- Engaging in sustained participation
- Applying conflict management techniques
- Dealing with change
- Other:

Physical

- Maintaining acceptable personal appearance
- Managing physical/medical needs
- Mobility
- Manipulating materials and equipment
- Other:

Technology

- Demonstrating computer literacy
- Selecting technology appropriate to the situation
- Applying technology
- Using keyboard skills
- Using input devices (mouse)
- Accessing computer system
- Selecting and using appropriate software
- Using technology information
- Other:

Reprinted with permission from *Opportunities for All* (1996), Colorado Department of Education.

Appendix C

Cross-reference of Strategies Matched to Subject Areas

With this cross-reference, you can easily find strategies to meet needs in specific subjects. The subjects are listed alphabetically and the strategies are matched to the standards. But remember: Each strategy can be used in more ways than those listed here. Be creative!

Standard	Strategy	Page
	Lifelong Learning	
The student will ask for and accept support.	Making the Abstract Concrete With Colorful Cubes	**46**
The student will gain and apply study skills (visual searching).	"I Spy" Quilts for Language Acquisition	**52**
The student will demonstrate time management skills.	Interactive Learning With Match 'Em Up Books	**56**
	Powerful Review With Pegboards	**110**
The student will maintain attention to text material.	Boost Fluency With Colored Strips	**58**
The student will use effective oral communication skills in group activities.	Mastering Content With the Info Ball Game	**60**
The student will gain and apply study skills and learning strategies for managing self.	Improve Comprehension With Sticky Summaries	**66**
The student will demonstrate socially acceptable behavior.	Compare and Contrast With Hula Hoops	**70**
The student will attend to important details in printed text.	Increase Fluency and Comprehension by "Chunking"	**76**

More ➲

📖 Lifelong Learning (continued)

Standard	Strategy	Page
The student will use self-regulation techniques to enhance learning opportunities.	Improve Performance With Self-Monitoring Systems	80
The student will maintain energy and focus over a sustained period of time or activity.	Improve Visual Focus With Work Masks	106
The student will use structured and discretionary time in appropriate ways.	Powerful Review With Pegboards	110
The student will apply organizational and study skills across the content areas.	Cross-Discipline Writing and Note-Taking With Model Notebooks	114
The student will use a variety of strategies and tools to organize materials.	Touchy Subjects: Learning With Labelmakers	116
The student will act independently based on knowledge of personal needs and preferences.	Foster Independent Decision-Making With Color Dots	120
Standard:	Monitor Learning With Bead Counters	130

Mathematics

Standard	Strategy	Page
The student will recall basic addition facts, sums to 10 or less, and the corresponding subtraction facts.	Practicing Facts With Larry's "Laptop"	41
	Step Up to Mastery With Hop-Step Mats	92
	Increase Proficiency With "Name That Number"	112
The student will count by twos, fives, and tens to 100.	Strengthen Learning With Feedback Pipes	44
	Review Content With Inside/Outside Circles	98
The student will compare and convert units of measure for length, weight, and volume within the U.S. Customary system and with the metric system.	Independent Practice With Fact Flippers	54

More ➔

Standard	Strategy	Page
The student will use basic and advanced procedures while performing the processes of computation.	Mastering Content With the Info Ball Game	**60**
The student will round whole numbers to the nearest tens and hundreds.	Wake 'Em Up With Stepping Stones	**68**
The student will identify relevant properties of plane and solid geometric figures.	Wake 'Em Up With Stepping Stones	**68**
The student will demonstrate conceptual meanings for the operations of multiplication and division.	Make Math More Meaningful With Fact Family Triangles	**74**
The student will demonstrate proficiency with basic multiplication and division facts without the use of a calculator.	Make Math More Meaningful With Fact Family Triangles Increase Proficiency With "Name That Number"	**74** **112**
The student will recognize, draw, describe, and analyze geometric shapes in one, two, and three dimensions.	Help Students Find Answers With Grabbers	**86**
The student will make and use direct and indirect measurements to describe and compare objects in his or her environment.	Reading, Measuring, and Analyzing With Wikki Stix	**90**
The student will demonstrate understanding and proficiency with basic addition and subtraction.	Step Up to Mastery With Hop-Step Mats	**92**
The student will link concepts and procedures as he or she develops and uses computational techniques.	Neatness Counts! Try Graph Paper	**94**
The student will identify, describe, analyze, extend, and create a wide variety of patterns in numbers, shapes, and data.	Generalize Learning With Go-Together Puzzles	**96**
The student will use the relationships among numbers in problem-solving situations by comparing fractions, decimals, and percents.	Generalize Learning With Go-Together Puzzles	**96**

More ⟳

169

Mathematics (continued)

Standard	Strategy	Page
The student will demonstrate number sense by skip counting by twos, fives, and tens.	Review Content With Inside/Outside Circles	**98**
The student will select and apply appropriate computational techniques to solve a variety of word problems.	Differentiate Learning With Fold-and-Flips	**100**
The student will apply number theory concepts to represent numbers in various ways (e.g., primes, composites, factors, and multiples).	Make Question & Answer Periods More Fun With Fortune Tellers	**108**
The student will reproduce, extend, create, and describe patterns and sequences using a variety of materials.	Powerful Review With Pegboards	**110**
The student will demonstrate proficiency with basic addition, subtraction, multiplication, and division facts without the use of a calculator.	Increase Proficiency With "Name That Number"	**112**
The student will construct, use, and explain procedures used in problem-solving situations.	Increase Proficiency With "Name That Number"	**112**
The student will recognize and write numerals 0–100.	Touchy Subjects: Learning With Labelmakers	**116**
The student will know, use, and describe the advantages and disadvantages of a variety of problem-solving sequences.	Teach Time Lines, Methods, and Processes With Kinesthetic Sequencing	**122**
The student will represent and use numbers in a variety of equivalent forms.	Increase the Participation of *All* Your Students With "Numbered Heads Together"	**124**
Standard:	Monitor Learning With Bead Counters	**130**

Reading

Also see writing strategies in this appendix.

Standard	Strategy	Page
The student will demonstrate comprehension of a variety of literary forms, including fiction, nonfiction, and poetry.	Active Reading Using Highlighter Tape	42
	Make Clear Connections Between Concepts With Learning Links	102
The student will hear, say, and manipulate phonemes.	Strengthen Learning With Feedback Pipes	44
	"I Spy" Quilts for Language Acquisition	52
The student will reflect on what has been learned from reading.	Better Retention With Note-Taking Quilts	48
The student will read and learn the meanings of unfamiliar words.	Independent Practice With Fact Flippers	54
The student will apply knowledge of how print is organized and read.	Interactive Learning With Match 'Em Up Books	56
The student will apply word analysis skills to ensure proper grammar usage.	Interactive Learning With Match 'Em Up Books	56
The student will read aloud familiar stories, poems, and passages with fluency and expression (rhythm, flow, meter, tempo).	Boost Fluency With Colored Strips	58
	Increase Fluency and Comprehension by "Chunking"	76
The student will analyze and evaluate information from a variety of sources.	Expand Thinking With "Roll the Cube"	62
The student will paraphrase information found in nonfiction materials.	Improve Comprehension With Sticky Summaries	66
The student will independently read and follow detailed directions in paragraph form.	Increase Fluency and Comprehension by "Chunking"	76
The student will independently read with appropriate fluency to enhance comprehension.	Increase Fluency and Comprehension by "Chunking"	76

More ➲

171

Reading (continued)
Also see writing strategies in this appendix.

Standard	Strategy	Page
The student will use a variety of reading strategies to read and understand text.	Improve Performance With Self-Monitoring Systems	80
	Make Clear Connections Between Concepts With Learning Links	102
	Increase the Participation of *All* Your Students With "Numbered Heads Together"	124
	Encourage Active Reading With Bullet Bookmarks	126
The student will discriminate between fact and opinion when reading text.	Reading, Measuring, and Analyzing With Wikki Stix	90
The student will critically analyze and comprehend text by making connections to personal experience, other texts, and media.	Generalize Learning With Go-Together Puzzles	96
The student will read and respond to written works of differing genres.	Revitalize Review With Beach-Ball Response	104
The student will make and check predictions about a story by using cover, title, and pictures.	Improve Visual Focus With Work Masks	106
The student will compare and contrast story elements (characters, settings, events).	Make Question & Answer Periods More Fun With Fortune Tellers	108
The student will correctly use new vocabulary from literature in other contexts.	Make Question & Answer Periods More Fun With Fortune Tellers	108
The student will use a full range of strategies to comprehend fiction and nonfiction.	Increase the Participation of *All* Your Students With "Numbered Heads Together"	124
Standard:	Monitor Learning With Bead Counters	130

Science

Standard	Strategy	Page
The student will plan and conduct investigations in which unexpected or unusual quantitative data are recognized.	Active Reading Using Highlighter Tape	**42**
The student will understand biological evolution and the diversity of life.	Better Retention With Note-Taking Quilts	**48**
The student will understand and follow a process of scientific inquiry.	Organize Information With Graphic Organizers	**50**
The student will investigate and understand that organisms are made of cells and have distinguishing characteristics.	Teach Categorization Skills With the Silent Sort Game	**64**
The student will investigate and understand that objects can be described in terms of their physical properties.	Teach Categorization Skills With the Silent Sort Game	**64**
The student will compare and contrast results of various investigations.	Compare and Contrast With Hula Hoops	**70**
The student will investigate and understand that living things are part of a system and are interdependent with their living and nonliving surroundings.	Make Complex Concepts Easier to Understand With Symbol Blocks	**82**
The student will know the earth's composition and structure (and associated vocabulary).	Review Content With Inside/Outside Circles	**98**
The student will understand the various forms of energy.	Diversify Instruction With Music Videos	**118**
The student will know, use, and describe the advantages and disadvantages of a chosen scientific method.	Teach Time Lines, Methods, and Processes With Kinesthetic Sequencing	**122**
The student will investigate and understand how plants interact with their nonliving environment.	Increase the Participation of *All* Your Students With "Numbered Heads Together"	**124**
Standard:	Monitor Learning With Bead Counters	**130**

173

Social Studies

Standard	Strategy	Page
The student will develop historical analysis skills, including identifying, analyzing, and making generalizations using primary sources.	Active Reading Using Highlighter Tape	42
The student will explain how massive immigration transformed American life.	Better Retention With Note-Taking Quilts	48
The student will describe how specific decisions and events had an impact on history.	Organize Information With Graphic Organizers	50
The student will know the location of places and geographic features.	Mastering Content With the Info Ball Game	60
The student will describe the ideas and events of the 1920s, 1930s, and 1940s in the United States.	Wake 'Em Up With Stepping Stones	68
The student will compare his or her own state to states from various regions of the country.	Compare and Contrast With Hula Hoops	70
The student will explain the fundamental ideals and principles that form the foundation of our government.	Make Complex Concepts Easier to Understand With Symbol Blocks	82
The student will describe the U.S. as composed of states and locate and name states in his or her own geographic region.	Teach Structures Kinesthetically With the Powder Walk	84
The student will analyze historical text and identify key dates and events in state history.	Reading, Measuring, and Analyzing With Wikki Stix	90
The student will differentiate between historical fact and folklore.	Powerful Review With Pegboards	110
The student will understand that people in the United States and Canada can influence the action and decisions of their governments through voting.	Foster Independent Decision-Making With Color Dots	120
The student will know how to construct time lines using months, years, decades, and centuries.	Teach Time Lines, Methods, and Processes With Kinesthetic Sequencing	122
Standard:	Monitor Learning With Bead Counters	130

Writing

Also see Reading strategies in this appendix.

Standard	Strategy	Page
The student will write to communicate ideas, using correct spelling for frequently used words.	Practicing Facts With Larry's "Laptop"	41
	Teach Spelling and Vocabulary With Sign and Spell	72
	Develop Automaticity With Musical Spelling	78
	Step Up to Mastery With Hop-Step Mats	92
	Touchy Subjects: Learning With Labelmakers	116
The student will write descriptive paragraphs, editing for proper grammar.	Making the Abstract Concrete With Colorful Cubes	46
The student will write for a variety of purposes, organizing information to fit the purpose.	Organize Information With Graphic Organizers	50
The student will expand and use vocabulary to describe people, places, and things.	"I Spy" Quilts for Language Acquisition	52
The student will write descriptive paragraphs that elaborate on the central idea.	Expand Thinking With "Roll the Cube"	62
The student will organize ideas in a logical manner.	Teach Categorization Skills With the Silent Sort Game	64
The student will correctly spell frequently used words.	Teach Spelling and Vocabulary With "Sign and Spell"	72
The student will write for a variety of purposes, selecting vocabulary to enhance the central idea and voice.	Teach Spelling and Vocabulary With "Sign and Spell"	72
The student will accurately use spelling words (district grade level list) in writing.	Develop Automaticity With Musical Spelling	78
The student will add or substitute sentences to clarify and enhance meaning.	Improve Performance With Self-Monitoring Systems	80
The student will be able to identify the parts of speech, such as nouns, pronouns, verbs, adverbs, adjectives, conjunctions, prepositions, and interjections.	Help Students Find Answers With Grabbers	86

More ➲

Appendix C: Cross-reference of Strategies Matched to Subject Areas

175

Meeting Standards

Writing (continued)

Also see Reading strategies in this appendix.

Standard	Strategy	Page
The student will be able to write stories, letters, and reports with greater detail and supporting material.	Improve Writing Skills With Light Pens	88
The student will be able to create documents with legible handwriting.	Improve Writing Skills With Light Pens	88
	Neatness Counts! Try Graph Paper	94
The student will edit and revise written work.	Improve Writing Skills With Light Pens	88
The student will organize written work using strategies such as lists, outlining, and appropriate graphic representations.	Step Up to Mastery With Hop-Step Mats	92
The student will spell frequently used words correctly, using phonics rules and exceptions.	Step Up to Mastery With Hop-Step Mats	92
The student will create readable documents with legible handwriting.	Neatness Counts! Try Graph Paper	94
The student will write, using conventional grammar, sentence structure, punctuation, capitalization, and spelling.	Differentiate Learning With Fold-and-Flips	100
The student will generate topics and develop ideas for a variety of writing purposes.	Make Clear Connections Between Concepts With Learning Links	102
	Foster Independent Decision-Making With Color Dots	120
The student will use writing as a tool for learning in all subjects (making lists, paraphrasing, summarizing, and synthesizing).	Cross-Discipline Writing and Note-Taking With Model Notebooks	114
The student will use correct spelling for frequently used words.	Touchy Subjects: Learning With Labelmakers	116
The student will generate writing topics and develop ideas using prewriting techniques.	Foster Independent Decision-Making With Color Dots	120

More ➲

Writing (continued)

Also see Reading strategies in this appendix.

Standard	Strategy	Page
The student will use a variety of writing strategies to gather and organize information.	Encourage Active Reading With Bullet Bookmarks	**126**
Standard:	Monitor Learning With Bead Counters	**130**

Other Areas

Standard	Strategy	Page
Art: The student will know how ideas and emotions are expressed through visual arts.	Improve Visual Focus With Work Masks	**106**
Foreign Language: The student will use the target language to engage in conversations.	Strengthen Learning With Feedback Pipes	**44**
Foreign Language: The student will use basic vocabulary to describe items in the environment.	"I Spy" Quilts for Language Acquisition	**52**
Health: The student will know the basic structure of the human body.	Teach Structures Kinesthetically With the Powder Walk	**84**
Health: The student will use various strategies for responding to negative peer influences.	Make Clear Connections Between Concepts With Learning Links	**102**
Music: The student will demonstrate understanding of the relationships among music, history, and culture.	Revitalize Review With Beach-Ball Response	**104**
Physical Education: The student will participate in activities that develop physical endurance.	Improve Performance With Self-Monitoring Systems	**80**
Technology: The student will know the characteristics and uses of computer hardware and operating systems.	Practicing Facts With Larry's "Laptop"	**41**
Technology: The student will know characteristics and uses of a computer's special function keys.	Independent Practice With Fact Flippers	**54**

More ➦

Other Areas (continued)

Standard	Strategy	Page
Technology: The student will demonstrate a basic understanding of computer theory.	Diversify Instruction With Music Videos	**118**
Standard:	Monitor Learning With Bead Counters	**130**

Where to Purchase Materials

Colored Acetate

⟳ Classroom Direct
www.classroomdirect.com
(800) 599-3040

Highlighter Tape

⟳ Lee Products, Minneapolis, MN
(800) 989-3544

⟳ Crystal Springs Publishing
(800) 321-0401

Quick "I Spy" Quilt Kit

⟳ Seaport Fabrics
www.seaportfabrics.com/quilts.htm

Nite Companion Pen Light

⟳ A & W Products Co., P.O. Box B, 14 Gardner St., Port Jervis, NY 12771
(845) 856-5156

Unifix Cubes

⟳ Didax, 395 Main St., Rowley, MA 01969
(800) 458-0024
www.didaxinc.com/unifix/html

Wikki Stix

⟳ The Wikki Stix Company, Omnicor, Inc., Phoenix, AZ
(800) TO-WIKKI

References

Anderson, K. 2001. Voicing concern about noisy classrooms. *Educational Leadership,* 58(7): 77–79.

Barron, B., M. Henderson, and R. Spurgeon 1994. Effects of time of day instruction on reading achievement of below grade readers. *Reading Improvements,* 31(1): 56–60.

Baum, L. F. 2001. *The wizard of oz.* New York: Scholastic.

Beninghof, A. 1998. *SenseAble strategies: Including diverse learners through multisensory strategies.* Longmont, CO: Sopris West.

Beninghof, A. and A. Singer 1995. *Ideas for inclusion: The school administrator's guide.* Longmont, CO: Sopris West.

Brimberry, A. 1996. Meeting individual differences through school study teams. *Equity and Excellence in Education,* 29: 30–33.

Calhoun, E. 1999. The singular power of one goal. Interview by Dennis Sparks in *Journal of Staff Development,* Winter: 54–57.

Callan, R. 1998. Giving students the right time of day. *Education Leadership,* December/January: 84–87.

Carbo, M. 1994. *Reading style inventory.* New York: National Reading Styles Institute.

Carbo, M., R. Dunn, and K. Dunn 1991. *Teaching students to read through their individual learning styles.* Boston: Allyn and Bacon.

DuFour, R. 2000. Clear connections. *Journal of Staff Development,* 21(2): 59–60.

Dunn, R. 1996. *How to implement and supervise a learning style program.* Alexandria, VA: Association for Supervision and Curriculum Development.

Dunn, R., K. Dunn, and G. Price 1997. Diagnosing learning styles: Avoiding malpractice suits against school systems. *Phi Delta Kappan,* 58(5): 418–420.

Dunn, R., K. Dunn, and G. Price 1994. *Learning style inventory.* Lawrence, KS: Price Systems.

Easton, L. 2000. If standards are absolute… . *Education Week,* 12 April, 50.

Education Week. 2000. XX(13): 14, November 29.

Eisner, E. 1993. Why standards may not improve schools. *Educational Leadership,* 50(5).

Ferrandino, V. and G. Tirozzi 2001. Test driven or data driven? *Education Week*, XX (37): 29.

Fullan, M. 1997. Broadening the concept of teacher leadership. In *Professional development in learning centered schools*. Edited by S. Caldwell. Oxford, OH: National Staff Development Council.

Gonzales, F. 1995. *Teaching content subjects to LEP students: 20 tips for teachers*. The Intercultural Development Research Association Newsletter, 22(2), 3: 16–17.

Governor's Task Force on Readiness 1987 Florida. As mentioned in ERIC Digest, Series 21: 2.

Holloway, J. 1999. Giving our students the time of day. *Education Leadership*, September: 87-88.

Joossee, B. M. 1996. *I love you the purplest*. San Francisco: Chronicle Books, 148.

Kagan, S. 1994. *Cooperative Learning*. San Clemente, CA: Kagan Publishing. www.kaganonline.com.

Kovaleski, J., E. Gickling, and H. Morrow 1999. High versus low implementation of instructional support teams: A case for maintaining program fidelity. *Remedial and Special Education*, 20(3): 170–83.

Marzano, R., B. Gaddy, and C. Dean 2000. *What works in classroom instruction*. McREL: Aurora, CO.

Marzollo, J. and W. Wick 1996. *I spy school days: A book of picture riddles*. New York: Scholastic.

McCarthy, B. 1993. *The learning type measure*. Barrington, IL: Excel.

McGraw Hill 2002. *Everyday mathematics: Student reference book fifth grade*. New York: Author.

Miles, K. and E. Guiney 2000. An answer to standards drumbeat. *Journal of Staff Development*, 21(4).

National Commission on Excellence in Education 1983. A nation at risk: The imperative for educational reform. Washington, DC: U.S. Government Printing Office.

National Education Goals Panel 1993. National education goals report. Washington, DC: U.S. Government Printing Office.

Nickols, F. 1994. Reengineering the problem solving process (finding better solutions faster). *Performance Improvement Quarterly*, 7(4): 3-19.

Osborne, A. 1963. *Applied imagination*. New York: Charles Scribner's Sons.

Polloway, E., W. Bursuck, M. Jaynthi, M. Epstein, and J. Nelson 1996. Treatment acceptability: Determining appropriate interventions within inclusive classrooms. *Intervention in School and Clinic*, 31: 133–44.

Riekehof, L. 1987. *The joy of signing*. Springfield, MO: Gospel Publishing.

Rowling, J. K. 1999. *Harry Potter and the sorcerer's stone*. New York: Scholastic.

Sapon-Shevin, M. 2001. Schools fit for all. *Education Leadership*, 58(4): 34–39.

Tomlinson, C. 2000. Reconcilable differences? Standards-based teaching and differentiaton. *Educational Leadership*, 58(1): 6–11.

Viadero, D. 2000. *Education Week*, 12 April.

Wenglinsky, H. 2000. *How teaching matters: Bringing the classroom back into discussions of teacher quality*. Princeton, NJ: Milken Family Foundation and the Educational Testing Service.

Other Publications of Interest
from Sopris West Educational Services

Sense*Able* Strategies

Including Diverse Learners Through Multisensory Strategies

Anne M. Beninghof

Grades PreK–6

Every day, teachers are faced with classes of students who demonstrate learning in a wide variety of ways. This book helps meet the challenge of this diversity of learning styles with classroom-tested, easy-to-implement methods for teaching through the four modalities (visual, auditory, tactile, and kinesthetic), paying special attention to the often-underutilized tactile and kinesthetic modalities.

In addition to providing practical, creative strategies that will help you reach all the students in your classroom, *Sense*Able *Strategies* provides:

- ➲ Guidelines for multisensory lesson planning and sample lesson plans
- ➲ Resources for assessment of learning styles
- ➲ Support for involving families in a learning styles program
- ➲ Ideas for teaching students about learning styles
- ➲ Reproducibles that support effective implementation

Item number: 53STRAT

More ➲

Ideas for Inclusion

The Classroom Teacher's Guide to Integrating Students
With Severe Disabilities

Anne M. Beninghof

Grades K–12

Include All the Kids in Your Classroom Simply and Effectively

Beninghof's good teaching ideas have helped many, many learners—with wide-ranging abilities—achieve. Now you can maximize individual learning and achievement in your own classroom with these 50 strategies that cut across disability categories. Revised to include IDEA requirements, *Ideas for Inclusion* offers time-proven and easy-to-implement ideas that don't require large expenditures of time or money, and yet are highly effective. With *Ideas for Inclusion*, you will:

- ⮑ Bring about changes in student attitudes and behaviors
- ⮑ Promote learning through environmental adaptations
- ⮑ Organize materials, schedules, and assignments for success
- ⮑ Differentiate instruction for individual learning styles
- ⮑ Work more effectively with paraeducators
- ⮑ Facilitate student friendships and social adjustment
- ⮑ Reduce disruptive behaviors through assessment and planning
- ⮑ Understand the legal and historical rationales for inclusion that every teacher should know
- ⮑ Heighten student motivation using cooperative learning, and much more

Item number: 53IDEAS

184

Ideas for Inclusion

The School Administrator's Guide

Anne M. Beninghof and Anne Louise T. Singer

Grades K–8

As educational leaders, school administrators play a crucial role in developing and nurturing the values and culture of the schools and districts in which they work. It is therefore essential that administrators possess the understanding and skills to ensure that their schools become places where all students are provided with an appropriate and useful education. *Ideas for Inclusion: The School Administrator's Guide* offers solutions to the common obstacles faced by administrators as they work to realize a truly inclusive environment for their students.

Ideas for Inclusion provides numerous strategies for examining and enacting positive change in the areas of:

- ⟳ **Leadership**—Sharing a Vision and Preparing the Way for Its Realization

- ⟳ **Planning Processes**—Drawing the "Map" to Successful Inclusion

- ⟳ **Assessment**—Collecting Data to Ensure Continuing Improvement

- ⟳ **Curriculum and Instruction**—Developing IEPs, Modifications, and More

- ⟳ **Student Supports**—Enlisting Peers and Community Resources to Enhance Integration Success

- ⟳ **Family and Community**—Fostering Communication and Cooperation

- ⟳ **Business Management**—Making the Most of Fiscal, Facility, and Transportation Resources

- ⟳ **Personnel**—Maximizing Human Resources Through Role Clarification, Staffing Patterns, and Evaluation

Ideas for Inclusion: The School Administrator's Guide was developed in part due to the success of its companion piece, *Ideas for Inclusion: The Classroom Teacher's Guide to Integrating Students With Severe Disabilities*. By utilizing both of these highly practical resources, administrators and the teachers with whom they work will be better prepared to successfully meet the challenges of creating truly inclusive schools.

185

Item number: 53ADMIN

Making Inclusion Work
Video and Facilitator's Guide
Anne M. Beninghof

Develop your inclusion skills with this video of practical strategies for teaching diverse learners, effective collaborative teaching methods, and planning guidelines. Featuring Anne M. Beninghof, nationally recognized consultant and trainer, this video provides creative, practical ideas for making inclusion work. The accompanying Facilitator's Guide offers ideas for using *Making Inclusion Work* with groups and individual regular classroom teachers, special education teachers, paraprofessionals, staff developers, administrators, and related professionals.

Item number: 121MIW

379.158 Ben
Beninghof, Anne M.
Meeting standards
fxc03002651

Education Library
Sprague Technology Center

Education Library
Sprague Technology Center